Groupe de Con

Les Cigognes

France's Ace Fighter Group in World War 1

Jon Guttman
Series editor Tony Holmes

Front Cover
At 1110 hrs on 7 July 1917, Capitaine Georges Guynemer of N3 shot down Albatros D III 1997/16 in flames over Villers-Franqueux, killing Ltn Reinhold Oertelt of *Jasta* 19. At 1230 hrs that afternoon he brought down an Aviatik C IV (a licence-built version of the DFW C V) near Moussy, killing its observer, Ltn Walter Ghers of *Flieger Abteilung* (A) 280. These successes, which boosted the French ace's score to 48, were the last he would achieve in the SPAD VII. Guynemer was flying S413 on this occasion, the SPAD scout being among the least decorative machines to be assigned to him. Indeed, it bore only his number 2 on the right upper wing, a white stork with black wing and tail feathers on the fuselage sides and a black leader's pennant on the upper decking. Guynemer scored six confirmed victories with S413 before switching to the more advanced SPAD XII and XIII (*Cover artwork by Mark Postlethwaite*)

First published in Great Britain in 2004 by Osprey Publishing
1st Floor Elms Court, Chapel Way, Botley, Oxford, OX2 9LP

© 2004 Osprey Publishing Limited

ISBN 1 84176 753 0

Edited by Tony Holmes
Page design by Mark Holt
Cover Artwork by Mark Postlethwaite
Aircraft Profiles by Harry Dempsey
Index by Alan Thatcher
Origination by Grasmere Digital Imaging, Leeds, UK
Printed in Hong Kong through Bookbuilders

04 05 06 07 08   10 9 8 7 6 5 4 3 2 1

ACKNOWLEDGEMENTS
Thanks to those colleagues whose invaluable assistance in the 'scavenger hunt' for photographs and supplementary information made this book what it is: Frank W Bailey, August G Blume, Jack Eder, Norman L R Franks and Greg VanWyngarden. Thanks also to the late Joseph Henri Guiguet, Alfred Heurteaux and especially Louis Risacher, for their helpful comments on GC12. This book is dedicated to their memory – and to their comrades-in-flight.

EDITOR'S NOTE
To make this series as authoritative as possible, the Editor would be interested in hearing from any individual who may have relevant photographs, documentation or first-hand experiences relating to the world's elite units, their pilots and their aircraft, of the various theatres of war. Any material used will be credited to its original source. Please contact Tony Holmes via e-mail at: tony.holmes@osprey-jets.freeserve.co.uk

For details of all Osprey Publishing titles please contact us at:

Osprey Direct UK, PO Box 140, Wellingborough, Northants NN8 2FA, UK
E-mail: **info@ospreydirect.co.uk**

Osprey Direct USA c/o MBI Publishing, PO Box 1, 729 Prospect Ave, Osceola, WI 54020, USA
E-mail: **info@ospreydirectusa.com**

Or visit our website: **www.ospreypublishing.com**

CONTENTS

BIRDS OF A FEATHER

In the autumn of 1918 the Allies were finally, definitively on the offensive after four years of agonising, trench-bound stalemate. At the airfield at La Noblette, SPAD XIII fighter aeroplanes, their fuselage sides adorned with storks in various attitudes of flight, prepared for the day's next patrol. The storks signified that these were aircraft of *Groupe de Combat* (GC) 12, the most successful fighter unit in the *Aviation Militaire*, and whose personnel included some of the most renowned names in French military aviation, alive and dead.

Among the still-living legends who were preparing for just another day's work over the front was the group's top scorer, Lt René Fonck. At age 24, this physically unimposing young man from the Vosges region had 60 victories to his credit, and his greatest days were by no means behind him. 'A big road ran through our landing field', he wrote in his post-war biography, 'and suddenly a returning column of *poilus* appeared. They were the remnants of the 26th Infantry, and they were moving slowly, painfully, as though they scarcely had the strength to drag themselves forward. The first ranks lined up instinctively in order to give the illusion of a force still intact – but behind them was dragging a lamentable motley crew of soldiers, covered with mud, with drawn, haggard features and feverish eyes.

'As for the officers, there were hardly any left. I saw only two at the head of the troops. They seemed like they were emerging from a tomb. They were heroes! They had attacked, counterattacked, held their ground against bayonets, grenades and gas. If they moved back to regroup, it was because their resistance had reached the limits of human endurance.'

As the soldiers plodded along, their captain recognised the stork insignias on the sides of the aeroplanes. Word passed down the line and the long-suffering ground troops who had borne the brunt of the Great War squared their shoulders and held their heads high, as if passing in review. A bugle played some appropriate notes and the men marched on while the airmen observed. The fighter pilots may have enjoyed more publicity, but at this moment the respect between these fighting men, air and ground, was mutual.

As the *poilus* moved on, Fonck recognised some Parisian accents as passing troops good-naturedly commented, 'We know you fellows – we've seen you at work.'

'There were also some old men among them,' Fonck recalled. 'One of them, upon seeing us, was struck by our youth, and remarked in surprise, "Why, they are all kids!"'

As the powers involved in World War 1 began to take the aeroplane seriously as a source of intelligence, work began in earnest to turn it into a weapon capable of protecting the reconnaissance aeroplanes of one side while denying the sky to those of the other. By the end of 1915 the single-seat fighter had proven itself, either by means of a machine gun mounted above the upper wing, as on the French Nieuport 11 Bébé, by mounting the engine in the back, as on Britain's de Havilland DH 2, or by using various synchronising mechanisms to interrupt the weapon's fire whenever the propeller was in front of it, as on Germany's Fokker E I. With that established, the quest for aerial supremacy escalated from individual duels to forming squadrons, and later groups or wings, to achieve local superiority over a selected battlefront.

On 21 February 1916, Verdun became what France called its 'hinge of fate', as the German 5. *Armee*, commanded by Crown Prince Wilhelm und Knobelsdorf, assaulted the ancient city. Unknown to the French, seizing Verdun was only a secondary goal of the German offensive – its primary objective was to draw French units into a protracted battle of attrition that was meant to bleed them dry. The result would be months of seemingly pointless slaughter on the ground, while at the same time both sides struggled with equal ferocity for control of the air.

To counter the German *Flieger Abteilungen* (flying detachments), Fl. Abt. *(Artillerie)*, *Kampfgeschwader* (battle wings, or KG), *Kampfgeschwader der Oberstern Heeresleitung* (army command-directed battle wings, or *Kagohl*), as well as the Fokker-equipped *Kampfeinsitzer Kommandos,* or KEKs, formed to support them, *Chef des Escadrons* Jean Baptiste Marie Charles de Tricornot de Rose brought the best of the available *escadrilles de chasse*, or fighter squadrons – N12, N15, N31, N65, N67, N69, N124 and a detachment from N3 – into the Verdun sector.

Chef des Escadrons Jean Baptiste Marie Charles de Tricornot de Rose laid the groundwork for the *groupe de combat* in the spring of 1916, when he temporarily gathered *escadrilles de chasse* N12, N15, N31, N65, N67, N69, N124 and a detachment from N3 together in order to gain local air superiority over the Verdun sector. He was killed in an aeroplane crash on 11 May 1916, aged 49 (*Nick Mladenoff via Greg VanWyngarden*)

Adjutant Joseph-Henri Guiguet and groundcrewmen of *Escadrille* N3 prepare Nieuport 16 N939, regularly flown by Capt Félix Brocard, for a mission over Verdun in June 1916. To support the British Somme offensive in July, the aggressive Brocard commanded not only N3, but the *Groupement de Combat de la Somme*, comprising a grouping of N26, N37, N62, N65, N67, N73 and N103 (*Service Historique de l'Armée de l'Air (SHAA) B83.1173*)

Born on 14 November 1885, Félix Antonin Gabriel Brocard was a graduate of the Special Military School at St Cyr and a career officer who switched from infantry to flying in 1911. After instructing and commanding Deperdussin-equipped *escadrille* D6, he took command of MS3 on 21 March 1915 and led it actively and aggressively, mentoring a number of aces and scoring three victories of his own. Promoted to *chef de bataillon* on 16 October 1916, he assumed overall command of GC12, comprising *escadrilles* N3, N26, N73 and N103, when it officially commenced operations on 1 November 1916 (*Jon Guttman*)

By 16 April Nieuport and Morane Saulnier fighters, flying in flights of six or more, were overwhelming the Germans, who eventually responded by forming larger, more specialised, fighter units of their own known as *Jagdstaffeln* or *Jastas*. By the end of the year, neither side could claim absolute control of the air. On the ground, too, the struggle for Verdun remained in stalemate. Even as a battle of attrition, it had fallen short of German hopes, with French dead listed at 543,000, but their own side faring little better with more than 434,000 fatalities.

Meanwhile, on 1 July 1916, the British launched an offensive on the Somme River, which by November had also proven to be a bloody fiasco. Again, the French air service assembled its fighter units to support the effort, transferring N3, N65 and N67 to join N26, N37, N62, N103 and the newly formed N73. This time N3's commander, Capitaine Félix Antonin Gabriel Brocard, took charge of all the squadrons making up the *Groupement de Combat de la Somme*.

The success of the temporarily grouped *escadrilles de chasse* in both the Verdun and Somme campaigns led to a French decision to form permanent *groupes de combat*, and one of the first units so designated was GC12, on 16 October 1916. Commanded by Brocard, who was promoted to the temporary rank of *Chef de Bataillon*, GC12 comprised his old unit, the already famous N3, under Lt Alfred Heurtaux, N26, commanded by Capitaine Victor Ménard, N73, led by Lt Jean Richard, and N103 under Capitaine Jean d'Harcourt. The group officially commenced operations from Cachy aerodrome on 1 November 1916.

From then on, two factors would make GC12 one of the most renowned flying formations of World War 1. In the months that followed, the group would adopt variations on N3's stork insignia – inspired by the storks that nested in the chimney tops of Alsace-Lorraine – as a common emblem for all their aircraft. The other was that the group shot down more enemy aeroplanes, and concentrated more heroes and top-scoring aces within its rolls, than any comparable fighter organisation in the *Aviation Militaire*.

The nucleus, heart and soul of GC12 was *escadrille* N3. First formed with Blériot XI monoplanes as Bl3 in July 1912, the squadron initially saw wartime service in the Vosges region. On 15 March 1915, 29-year-old Capitaine Brocard, a 1907 graduate from the Special Military School at

St Cyr, took command, and three days later, the acquisition of Morane Saulnier L parasol monoplanes led to a change of designation as MS3.

On 3 July Brocard scored MS3's first aerial victory when he attacked an Albatros two-seater of Fl. Abt. 2 over Dreslincourt and, though armed only with a carbine, brought it down, killing the observer. A second success occurred on 19 July, when Cpl Georges Guynemer went up in a Morane Saulnier L with an improvised machine gun mount in the rear cockpit, manned by his mechanic, Soldat Jean Guerder. The pair shot

This remarkable collection of portrait photographs shows some of the pilots who contributed to the fame of the original 'Escadrille des Cigognes', N3. They are from left to right, upper row, Adjutant André Hénin, Lt Gustave Lagache, Lt Max Benoît (squadron technical assistant from 1 November 1916 to 22 February 1917), Capitaine Alfred Heurtaux, Commandant Félix Brocard, Capitaine Georges Guynemer, Capitaine Alfred Auger and Sous-Lt Henri Rabatel. Lower, row, from left to right, Sous-Lt Louis Bucquet, Adjutant Joseph Guiguet, Lt Mathieu Tenant de la Tour, Sous-Lt René Dorme, Lt Albert Deullin, Adjutant Célestin Sanglier and Adjutant Roger Guillaumot (*Louis Risacher Collection via Jon Guttman*)

N3's Sous-Lt Charles Louis de Guibert and Commandant Brocard with a SPAD VII (*Louis Risacher album via Jon Guttman*)

down an Aviatik between the lines, killing Uffz August Ströbel and Ltn Werner Johannes of Fl. Abt. 26.

Born in Paris on 24 December 1894, Georges Marie Ludovic Jules Guynemer was the third child of Paul Guynemer, a graduate of the military academy at St Cyr who had served in the French army until 1880, and married in 1890. In contrast to his two elder sisters, Georges was a sickly child, though his health gradually improved under his mother's care. After studying at home with his sisters, he attended the Lycée of Compiègne at age 14, but did poorly. When his father enrolled him at Stanislas College, however, Georges' academic record improved markedly. His headmaster's favourable report in the first term also described him as having a wilful nature, and noted that he 'is not particularly good at sports but shows promise in the College's small bore rifle shooting competition'.

At about the same time, a visit with a friend to the Panhard motor factory left Guynemer with a fascination for engines and all things mechanical. When a friend of his father's took him up for a 20-minute flight in a Farman in 1911, Georges regarded it as the thrill of a lifetime, and declared that from then on his ambition was to become a pilot. He graduated from Stanislas College with honours in 1912, but illness compelled him to take a long rest in southern France.

When war broke out, Guynemer promptly tried to enlist in the *Aviation Militaire*, but was rejected three times due to his poor health. On the fourth attempt he was finally accepted, and trained to be a mechanic at Pau aerodrome. Upon his arrival there on 23 November 1914, however, Guynemer applied for pilot training, and eventually his

The already celebrated Sgt Georges Guynemer prepares for a mission in July 1916. Unlike most of his other aircraft, Nieuport 17 N1531 does not bear his legend *'Le Vieux Charles'* on the fuselage, but instead carries it in white on black pennants attached to the interplane struts (*SHAA B88.353*)

persistence was rewarded on 10 March 1915, when he earned military pilot's brevet No 1832. Promoted to caporal on 8 May, Guynemer was assigned to MS3 exactly one month later. From their first flight over the lines on 10 June, Guynemer's observer, Guerder, noted that the new pilot seemed to have no fear of enemy gunfire, either from the ground or in the air. Indeed, the occasional rifle shots sent his way by the observers of the German aircraft encountered only inspired Guynemer to devise the aft gun mount for his Morane Saulnier.

After their combat of 19 July Guynemer and Guerder landed to obtain confirmation, and were interviewed by the commander of the 238e *Régiment*, whose soldiers had witnessed the action. 'Well, really the pilot did the whole thing,' Guerder said modestly, just as Guynemer entered the tent. Upon learning that the victorious gunner was 22 and his pilot only 20, the colonel burst into an exclamation that the airmen would hear often in the years to come. 'Don't we have anybody but children left to fight the war with?' Three days later Guynemer and Guerder received official confirmation of their success, both were awarded the *Médaille Militaire* and Guynemer was subsequently promoted to sergent.

Later in July, MS3 became one of the first squadrons to receive Nieuport 10 two-seaters. The unit moved from Vauciennes to Breuil-le-Sec on 16 August, and on the 28th Brocard shot down an enemy aeroplane north of Senlis.

By 20 September the *escadrille* was almost completely re-equipped with Nieuport sesquiplanes, and was officially redesignated N3. Its next success occurred on 5 December, when Guynemer took off in a modified single-seat Nieuport 10 with a Lewis infantry gun, complete with stock, mounted above the wing and brought down an Aviatik over Bois de Carré. Guynemer struck again on 8 December, shooting down an LVG between Roye and Nesle, killing Vzfw Kurt Diesendahl and Ltn Hans Reitter of Fl. Abt. 27. On 14 December Guynemer teamed up with a two-seater Nieuport 10, crewed by Adjutant André Bucquet and Sous-Lt Louis André Adolphe Pandevant, in downing a Fokker Eindecker over Hervilly.

Early in 1916 single-seat Nieuport 11 Bébés began to replace the Nieuport 10s. Guynemer received Nieuport 11 N836, on the fuselage of which he applied the legend *'Le Vieux Charles'*, a reference to Sgt Charles Bonnard, a well-liked member of old MS3 who had transferred to the Macedonian front.

Guynemer was flying that aeroplane on 3 February when he encountered an LVG near Roye. 'I did not open fire until I was at 20 metres,' Guynemer later wrote. 'Almost at once my adversary tumbled into a tailspin. I dived after him, continuing to fire my weapon. I plainly saw him fall in his own lines. That was all right. No doubt about him. I had my fifth. I was really in luck, for less than ten minutes later another aeroplane, sharing the same lot, spun downward with the same grace, taking fire as it fell through the clouds.'

German records documented only one fatality from the combat – Ltn Heinrich Zwenger, an observer of Fl. Abt. 27, killed between Roye and Chaulnes – but both LVGs were confirmed as the first double victory scored by a French airman. Guynemer added a seventh to his growing tally on 5 February with an LVG downed at Herbecourt, again killing the observer, Ltn Rudolf Lumblatt of Fl. Abt. 9. On 12 March Brocard led a

This Nieuport 17, flown by Capitaine Alfred Auger of N3 at Villers Bretonneux in October 1916, retains the green and brown camouflage and overwing Lewis gun mounting that were features of early production examples of the ubiquitous fighter (*SHAA B83.5654*)

Guynemer runs up SPAD VII S115 at Buc aerodrome in September 1916. Although he would not fly this particular machine for long, it sold him on the SPAD, which soon eclipsed the Nieuports both in N3 and throughout GC12 (*SHAA B88.542*)

detachment of pilots to Verdun, leaving Capitaine René Colomb in charge of most of N3 until 16 April, when the entire *escadrille* moved to Cachy in anticipation of the Somme offensive.

N3 received its first Nieuport 17s in June 1916, and in late August the unit got its first examples of a conceptually new fighter, the SPAD 7.C1. Developed by Louis Béchereau of the *Societé anonyme pour l'Aviation et ses dérivés*, the SPAD VII's sturdy airframe was mated to the newly developed 150-hp Hispano-Suiza 8Aa engine, and armed with a synchronised 0.30-calibre Vickers machine gun. Assigned SPAD VII S115 on 2 September, Sous-Lt Guynemer used it to down an Aviatik C II over Hyencourt for his 15th victory two days later, his victims being Ltns Hans Steiner and Otto Fresenius of *Kampfstaffel* 37.

Twenty-four SPAD VIIs reached the front in the course of September, and N3's aces, who had already mastered the manoeuvrable, but tricky Nieuports, quickly amended their tactics to take advantage of the new fighter's speed.

This rare in-flight photograph shows Guynemer on patrol over Verdun in SPAD S115 in September 1916. The aeroplane was brought down on 23 September 1916 in error by French anti-aircraft fire and subsequently demolished by souvenir-hungry *poilus* (*SHAA B77.1365*)

Second only to Guynemer in N3's ranks was Adjutant René Dorme, whose insatiable lust for revenge against the Germans for their occupation of Alsace and Lorraine drove him to score 23 confirmed victories, with at least as many again unconfirmed, about which he showed no concern (*Greg VanWyngarden*)

In five minutes on 23 September, Guynemer downed two Fokkers, plus a third that went unconfirmed, but as he returned over the lines at an altitude of 3000 metres, his new aeroplane was struck by a 75 mm shell fired by nervous French anti-aircraft gunners. With the water reservoir shattered and fabric torn away from his left upper wing, Guynemer spun down, but he managed to regain control and pull up at about 180 metres altitude, after which he crash-landed in a shell hole, emerging with a cut knee and a slight concussion. 'Only the fuselage was left, but it was intact,' he wrote in a letter to his father. 'The SPAD is solid – with another aeroplane, I would now be thinner than this piece of paper.' Sold on the new fighter, he was back in action in SPAD VII S132 two days later.

By 1 November, N3 had been credited with 65 enemy aircraft shot down for the loss of three pilots, two observers and one gunner killed in action, and two pilots and two observers missing. Guynemer then had 18 victories to his credit, and five of his squadronmates, René Dorme, André Chainat, Alfred Heurtaux, Albert Deullin and Mathieu Tenant de la Tour, were also aces of considerable renown.

Born in Baucourt-les-Souppleville, Meuse, on 30 January 1894, René Pierre Marie Dorme was serving in the *7e Groupe d'Artillerie á Pied* in

13

Lt Alfred Heurtaux was another early recipient of the SPAD VII at N3. The aircraft shown here may be his first assigned machine, S113 (*SHAA B76.1864*)

Bizerte, Tunisia, when World War 1 began, and he promptly requested a transfer into aviation. His first combat occurred while flying Caudron G IVs with *escadrille* C94, which cited him for probably shooting down a German aeroplane on 13 March 1916.

After being transferred to fighters with N3, the aggressive Dorme expressed his desire to liberate the territory occupied by the Germans after the 1870–71 Franco-Prussian War by marking a cross of Lorraine on his aircraft. His hatred for the enemy, however, never got the better of his judgement, and his relative maturity in combat gained him the nickname of '*Père* Dorme', which he also obligingly marked below his cockpit. After teaming up with Lt Alfred Heurtaux in shooting down an LVG on 9 July – credited as the first confirmed victory for both pilots – Dorme was awarded the *Médaille Militaire*. By 18 October, when he was made a *Chevalier de la Légion d'Honneur*, his score stood at 15 confirmed and seven probable victories in 86 combats, and a total of only 198 flying hours over the front.

First assigned to the artillery in 1913, André Julien Chainat was posted to Bl4 on 20 July 1913, and after pilot training he was transferred to MS23 and MS38, before joining N3 on 17 January 1916. He scored his first victory on 1 March, and by the end of October Adjutant Chainat had 11 – including two on 2 August, one of which was shared with Lt Heurtaux – as well as the *Croix de Guerre* with nine palms and one bronze star, the *Médaille Militaire* and the *Légion d'Honneur*.

Alfred Heurtaux was born in Nantes on 20 May 1893, and was a graduate of the military academy at St Cyr, gaining his commission with the *9e Régiment d'Hussards* in 1914. Deciding that the Western Front was no place for light cavalry, he entered aviation on 6 December, and after serving in MS26 as an observer, he earned his pilot's brevet on 29 May

1915. Assigned to MS38, Heurtaux was promoted to lieutenant on 25 December, and on 5 June 1916 he obtained a transfer to N3, assuming command of the squadron on 16 June. After his shared victory with Dorme, Heurtaux had become an ace and a *Chevalier de la Légion d'Honneur* by 17 August. Among his subsequent victories was a 'Fokker' over Villers Carbonnel on 25 September that turned out to have, in fact, been a Halberstadt D II flown by Ltn Kurt Wintgens of *Jagdstaffel* 1, an 18-victory ace and holder of the *Orden Pour le Mérite*. By 1 November Heurtaux's score stood at 10.

Albert Louis Deullin was born in Epernay on 24 August 1890 and entered the military at an early age. During the war, he served in the 31*e* and later the 8*e Régiment de Dragons*, was commissioned a sous-lieutenant in December 1914 and transferred to aviation in April 1915. Initially assigned to MF62 on 2 July, Deullin scored his first victory, with the aid of his observer, Capitaine Alphonse Colcomb, on 10 February 1916. He was transferred to N3 soon after that, and by the end of March 1916 he had two more enemy aeroplanes to his credit. He was wounded in combat on 2 April, but returned to action 15 days later and scored his fourth victory on the 30th, for which he was made a *Chevalier de la Légion d'Honneur* on 4 June. Deullin brought his total to eight on 22 September.

Born in Paris on 5 December 1883, Mathieu Marie Joseph Antoine Tenant de la Tour had been a cavalry officer before transferring to aviation. He first served in N57, burning a balloon on 25 January 1916 and being made a *Chévalier de la Légion d'Honneur* on 1 February. Wounded in action on 25 April, upon recovery he was reassigned to N3, where, flying Nieuports, he raised his score to five by 6 September.

N3's exploits had made *'les Cigognes'* (the Storks) a household word in France, and its insignia of a stork winging its way home toward Alsace

Lts Albert Deullin and Paul Tarascon stand beside Deullin's Nieuport 17 N1532 in the summer of 1916. Deullin already had eight victories to his credit by the time N3 became the nucleus of GC12 (*SHAA B76.1872*)

came to be recognised by its German adversaries as the harbinger of a tough fight to come. By the time GC12 was formed, the stork had become so associated with the *escadrille* that while it was stationed at Manoncourt, Hélène Herriot, wife of Edouard Herriot, mayor of Lyon, presented it with a live stork mascot.

Transporting the bird on the squadron's many shifts of venue proved to be impossible, so the pilots replaced it with a plush stuffed toy stork that stood on the mess table, facing welcome guests, or with its back turned to

Sous-Lt Georges Raymond, a future ace and commander of N3, peers from the cockpit of his Nieuport 17 in the autumn of 1916 (*SHAA B87.7102*)

Nieuport 17 N1538, bearing Raymond's usual number 9, a black command pennant on the fuselage upper decking and an unusual elliptical white or light blue highlight around the stork insignia, was flown by him in the autumn of 1916 (*SHAA B76.1872*)

visitors who were not. Named Hélène in *Madame* Herriot's honour, the inanimate mascot wore an *escadrille* lanyard around its neck, along with a placard proclaiming the unit's current victory tally. René Dorme was said to be especially fond of Hélène, and he carried it in his scout whenever the squadron moved, though it is less likely that he carried it in combat as some legends claimed. Hélène survived World War 1 and was preserved in a glass case, to carry on as mascot of *Groupe de Chasse* I/2 in the next war.

After 1945 the mascot was found to have deteriorated to the point that a replacement had to be made. That copy can currently be found at Airbase 102 at Dijon-Longvic, serving as mascot to N3's latest incarnation, *Escadrille de Chasse* 01/002.

When MS26 was formed at St Cyr on 26 August 1914, it had only four aircraft. Assigned to the Flanders sector on 21 September, the unit's first victory was scored by Sous-Lt Roland Garros, an already celebrated pre-war aviator who used a fixed Hotchkiss machine gun and steel deflectors behind the propeller blades to convert his Morane Saulnier L into the war's first single-seat fighter to see combat.

On 1 April, he used his ingenious, but dangerous, device to shoot down an Albatros two-seater over Westkappelle, probably killing Gftr August Spacholz and Lt Werner Grosskopf of Fl. Abt. 40. After an unconfirmed claim on 8 April, Garros downed an Aviatik between Ypres and Armenières on the 15th, probably killing Ernst Reuber of Fl. Abt. 11. He sent another Albatros crashing at Cortemarck on the 18th, but this time he caused so much damage to his own aeroplane that he was forced to land at Inglemunster, Belgium, and was taken prisoner. For three weeks Garros had been the terror of the sector, and the Germans were keen to copy his deflectors, but Anthony Fokker did that idea one better by fitting interrupter gear developed by Swiss engineer Franz Schneider to one of his Fokker monoplanes.

Re-equipped with Nieuports, MS26 was redesignated N26 on 20 September, and by the time it became part of GC12 it had accounted for 17 German aircraft and three balloons for the loss of one pilot killed, one missing, three wounded and five taken prisoner. Its only ace at that time

Pre-war pilot Roland Garros of N26 used steel wedges affixed to the back of the propeller blades of his Morane Saulnier L to allow him to mount a machine gun above the engine of his fighter. He then claimed three German aircraft destroyed in short order before he was himself brought down and taken prisoner in April 1915. He would later escape and return to SPA26 as part of GC12 (*Greg VanWyngarden*)

was Sous-Lt Noël de Rochefort, who downed seven enemy aeroplanes before being shot down behind German lines on 15 September and dying of his wounds the next day. The unit also had a future ace in Sgt Constant Roger Frédéric Soulier, who at age 19 already had an aeroplane and a balloon to his credit, as well as Lt Armand Pinsard.

Up to that time, Pinsard's principal claim to fame had been the result of his having been forced down in German territory on 8 February 1915, spending almost 14 months as a prisoner of war, then escaping with Capitaine Victor Ménard on 26 March 1916 and crossing the lines to safety on 10 April. Later assigned to N26, along with his co-escapee, who became its commander, Pinsard was the first frontline pilot to receive a SPAD VII in August 1916.

Another exceptional character in N26's ranks was its resident Japanese volunteer, Capitaine Kiyotake Shigeno. Born in Nagoya on 6 October 1882, Baron Shigeno sought a life of adventure after the untimely death of his young wife, Wakako, hoping to rejoin her soon through a heroic death

Lt Armand Pinsard and Capitaine Victor Raphaël Ménard after their escape from Swiss internment. Both pilots soon returned to action with N26, Ménard taking command of the *escadrille* in July 1916 (*SHAA B77.1391*)

of his own. Viewing the newly invented aeroplane as just the thing for a man seeking danger and glory, he moved to Paris, then the centre of aviation, in 1910. On 26 January 1912, he obtained International Pilot's Licence No 744, and by April he was flying a biplane of his own design, christened *Wakadori* in his wife's honour (*'dori'* means bird in Japanese).

When war broke out in Europe, Shigeno joined the 1*er Régiment Étranger* of the Foreign Legion, but he transferred to the air service on 20 December 1914. After serving for various lengths of time in *escadrilles* V22 and V27, he then joined V24. While most of Japan's wartime activities on the Allied side were devoted to seizing German possessions in the Pacific and besieging Germany's Chinese concession at Tsingtao, Shigeno was flying reconnaissance and bombing missions over the Western Front, earning citations for never failing to complete a mission, regardless of the intensity of enemy anti-aircraft fire, and often returning with his Voisin 3 riddled with projectiles.

On 28 September 1915 Shigeno made a *Chevalier de la Légion d'Honneur*, but in the following year he requested a change of venue to a fighter squadron. He was assigned to N12 on 1 June 1916, but two weeks later he was pulled out for fighter training and upon its completion he arrived at N26 on 17 September – as a replacement for the fallen Rochefort. Shigeno's first combat came on the 26th, and he was credited with his first victory, apparently shared with Ménard, on 16 October.

The next day, Shigeno almost got the glorious death he'd been seeking when he engaged a formation of Albatros fighters alone and his machine gun jammed. After a desperate struggle, he managed to extricate himself and make an emergency landing just inside French lines.

At the time of its permanent attachment to GC12, N26 had accounted for 17 enemy aircraft and three balloons, for the loss of one

Photographed having its gun sighted and the synchronisation gear adjusted in September 1916, Nieuport 17 N1804 displays the red star and pilot's roman numeral 'VIII' that typified N103's livery prior to its incorporation in GC12 (*SHAA B75.1290*)

Nieuport 17 N1521 still displayed the old livery of N26 after being passed on to the fighter training school at Avord in 1917. N26's torch insignia was replaced by a variation on N3's stork after it was incorporated into GC12 (*Jon Guttman*)

pilot killed, one missing, four brought down as prisoners, one interned in the Netherlands and three wounded. Of the PoWs, two died in captivity and one, Roland Garros, would later escape and rejoin the *escadrille*.

Formed from the *Détachement Nieuport de Corcieux* on 19 April 1916, N73 scored its first victory on 17 May, when Sgt Théophile Funck-Bretano and Cpl Robert Sabatier downed an Aviatik over Chatas. After downing another Aviatik five days later, Funck-Bretano became the unit's first casualty on 25 June when he was killed in combat with three German aircraft. After serving with the *Groupement de Combat de la Somme*, N73 was credited with three enemy aeroplanes destroyed and one forced to

Sgt Georges Lutzius runs through some pre-flight checks in the cockpit of a Nieuport 17 of N103 in September 1916. This early Nieuport 17 had a Lewis machine gun on an overwing mounting, rather than the more common synchronised Vickers (*SHAA B96.1276*)

land by November 1916, but it had lost one pilot killed, one missing, one wounded and one killed in a flying accident.

N103 had evolved from a bombing unit, being first mobilised on 2 August 1914 as Br17, equipped with Bréguet bombers. Re-equipped with Voisin 3s in November and assigned to *Groupe de Bombardment* 1, the squadron was redesignated VB3 on 5 January 1915, and again as VB103 on 25 May. The unit acquitted itself well in the bombing role, but on 19 February 1916 it was moved to Cachy, re-equipped with Nieuports and assigned to Brocard's *Groupement de Combat de la Somme* as N103.

The squadron's first victory was scored on 3 August by its commander, Capitaine Jean d'Harcourt, a 30-year-old Parisian-born career officer who

Sgt Lutzius' Nieuport 17 N1465 featured green and brown camouflage, a red star, white Roman numeral 'II', a cowling that may have been red and a blue *'cône de penetration'* (*SHAA B96.1287*)

Sgt Marcel Paris of N73 prepares to take off in his Nieuport 17, '*Boule de Neige*'. He was credited with shooting down one enemy aeroplane and forcing another to land prior to N73 being incorporated into GC12 (*SHAA B87.185*)

Capitaine Jean d'Harcourt alights from Nieuport 10 N496 at Grivesnes in January 1916. Victor over one enemy aeroplane, d'Harcourt led N103 until April 1918, when he was given command of GC13 (*SHAA B85.392*)

was already a *Chevalier de la Légion d'Honneur* from previous service in MS38. By 1 November the unit had five German aircraft to its credit, for the loss of six pilots and one bombardier in combat, and two pilots and one bombardier killed in accidents.

GC12 was not alone in its task. On the same day it was organised, GC13 was formed under *Chef de Bataillon* Philippe Féquant's command, made up of four other proven units – N65, N67, N112 and the American volunteer *escadrille* N124 (see Osprey Aviation Elite Units 17 - *SPA124 Lafayette Escadrille* for details). For the next two months, all of those units would operate together under the temporary designation *Groupe de Combat de Cachy*.

This line-up shot of early Nieuport 17s of N103 shows a mixed bag of cowlings – some annular, some replaced by Nieuport 11 cowls and two with non-rotating *'cônes de penetration'* (*SHAA B96.1285*)

INTO BATTLE IN GROUP STRENGTH

Hazy skies, wind and rain dampened GC12's first official day of operations – 1 November 1916 – but the group flew 12 sorties and had four aerial combats, as well as one pilot strafing German trenches near Chaules. At 1525 hrs that afternoon, Lt Pinsard opened the GC12's account when he drove an enemy aeroplane down to crash between Bus and Mesnil-en-Arrouaize. His first personal victory was also to be his last prior to leaving N26 to command N78 on 12 December. Pinsard would down another 15 Germans with that unit before being injured in a flying accident on 12 June 1917.

Upon his recovery, Pinsard took command of SPA23 early in 1918, raising his score to 27 on 22 August. Three days later he was made an *Officier de la Légion d'Honneur*, and by the end of the war he had also been awarded the *Croix de Guerre* with 19 palms and the British Military Cross. Pinsard continued to serve with distinction during World War 2, commanding *Groupe de Chasse* 21 until he was wounded in a bombing raid on 6 June 1940, resulting in the loss of a leg. Pinsard died in Ceyzeriat during a dinner being held by the *Les Vielles Tiges* association on 10 May 1953.

Cloudy weather again limited GC12 to 12 sorties on 2 November, although in the course of them it logged 16 inconclusive combats and its first casualty – Cpl Ravel of N103, whose Nieuport 21 failed to return from a patrol over the Chaulnes-le-Transloy area, and who was one of two Nieuports claimed by two-seater crews of *Kampfstaffel* 25 that day. On the 3rd, Heurtaux downed an Aviatik in flames over Rocquigny for his 11th victory, killing Uffz Ernst Hanold and Ltn Max Steiner of Fl. Abt. 42. In addition, Guynemer claimed a probable and Sgt Léonard Joseph Baron of N103 forced an enemy aeroplane to land.

On 6 November, Adjutant Weston Birch Hall of N103 damaged an enemy aeroplane over Buire. An American volunteer from Missouri, 'Bert' Hall had only joined the squadron five days earlier, having previously served in the Foreign Legion, *escadrille* MS38 and N124, the already famous *'Escadrille Américaine'*.

Hall was less well-to-do, older and more worldly than the young idealists who predominated in N124's ranks. With the exception of their leading ace, the equally worldly Gervais Raoul Lufbery, the Americans disliked Hall's crude language, continually questioned his honesty and suspected him of cheating at cards. Taking the hint that he was not welcome, Hall obtained a transfer to N103, but as he departed he allegedly shook his fist at the Americans and swore, 'You'll hear from me yet!' Hall already had two victories to his credit at N124, and his unconfirmed success of 6 November was only the first indication of his being as good as his word, at least in this case.

On the very day GC12 was formed, on 1 November 1916, Lt Armand Pinsard of N26 opened the group's account by downing an enemy aeroplane between Bus and Mesnil-en-Arrouaize. He failed to score again before leaving to take command of N78 on 12 December (*Jon Guttman*)

A former mechanic himself, Lieutenant Guynemer assists his groundcrewmen in working on the engine of SPAD VII S132 at Cachy in November 1916 (*SHAA 92.3739*)

Sgt Baron damaged a German aeroplane on the 8th, but on 9 November the weather cleared, allowing GC12 and GC13 to mount 30 patrols and fight 58 combats. Guynemer, Deullin, Bert Hall, Sgt Johannes Sauvage of N65 and Adjutant Lufbery and Sgt Paul Pavelka of N124 claimed a total of seven 'probables' that day, but the only confirmed victory went to Sous-Lt Auguste Ledeuil of N103. However, the latter unit lost Cpl Léon Millot, who was killed in action by either Ltn Walter Höhne or Ltn Hans Wortmann of *Jasta* 2.

The next day got off to an unpromising start when Sgt Marcel Bourdarie crashed his Nieuport 17 as N103 was taking off at 0630 hrs – he would die of his injuries on Christmas Day. Sgts Baron and Georges Lutzius damaged enemy aeroplanes at 0750 hrs, but neither could be confirmed. N73 took off 40 minutes later, but lost Sgt Roxas-Elias, whose Nieuport 21 was probably shot down by Oblt Erich Hahn of *Jasta* 1. At 1015 hrs, however, Maréchal-des-Logis (MdL) Soulier of N26 attacked five Aviatik two-seaters and, although riddled by their gunners, he sent 30 rounds into one and saw it descend in flames east of Péronne.

At 1215 hrs Guynemer spotted an Albatros C V being escorted by three Albatros scouts. Selecting the reconnaissance aeroplane first, he eliminated the observer with just three rounds, and another six killed the pilot. Ltn Karl Stämm and Albert Eder of Fl. Abt. 13 fell in French lines south of Nesle. Engaging the scouts, Guynemer sent one down in flames near Morcourt at 1225 hrs, probably killing Vzfw Christian Kress, a veteran pilot of *Jasta* 6 with four victories to his credit. That 'double' brought Guynemer's tally to 20, while Deullin scored his ninth victory at 1340 hrs.

GC12 dropped flechettes on reported enemy cavalry or horse-drawn vehicles on 10 and 11 November, and at 0900 hrs on the latter day Heurtaux downed an Albatros in flames over Saily-Saillisel, killing Uffz

Karl Münster and Ltn Max Hulse of *Kampfstaffel* 30/KG 5. In spite of high winds and bad weather, Cpl Sabatier of N73 scored his second victory on 12 November, and on the 15th, Adjutant Charles Jeronnez of N26 downed an Aviatik east of Chaulnes for his first success, killing Vzfw Hermann Michel and Oblt Heinrich Bauer of Fl. Abt. 7.

Heurtaux started 16 November off by destroying a scout east of Le Pressoire at 0930 hrs, killing Ltn Ernst Wever of *Jasta* 6. Guynemer downed a Fokker at 1340 hrs, Dorme sent a Rumpler down in flames east of Marchélepot at 1515 hrs and Sgt Jean Georges Sendral of N26 claimed a probable. GC12 seems to have made an impression on the Germans, for they bombed Cachy aerodrome that night, destroying N3's hangar and six of its aircraft, as well as damaging several aeroplanes from N26 and N65, killing Soldat Méchanicien Bessier and wounding seven others.

Adjutant François Bergot of N73 gained revenge by sending an enemy aeroplane down to crash in German lines the next day, but Bucquet's and Dorme's claims were not confirmed, and Sendral was wounded in action.

Weather curtailed operations until the 22nd, when Guynemer downed a Roland C II east of Saint-Christ at 1445 hrs. Fifteen minutes later he was jumped by four Halberstadts, but managed to turn the tables on his

This Nieuport 17 of N73 was left at this dramatic angle after suffering a landing mishap. The fighter displays the 'Japanese style' stork adopted by the unit after it became part of GC12 (*SHAA B90.80*)

25

assailants, and in the course of a long, running fight, shot one of them down between Falvy and Heilly and sent another one diving away. His confirmed victim in that mêlée was probably Gftr Robert Michaelis of *Jasta* 12, killed that day.

The 23nd saw Deullin send an adversary down in flames south of Bois de Vaux, killing Hptm Hans Linke and Ltn Wilhelm Steinbrenner of *Kampfstaffel* 25/KG 5. Bergot of N73 scored his second victory over Fins that morning and Ledeuil of N103 his third northeast of Marchélepot that afternoon. After a few days of bad weather, Bert Hall scored his third official victory on 26 November.

Following another week of poor flying weather, on 4 December Heurtaux and Dorme claimed Aviatiks that could not be confirmed, then Dorme took on two 'Fokkers' and destroyed one of them north of Saint Cren, killing Ofzr Karl Ehrenthaller of *Jasta* 1. On the 8th, Général Ferdinand Foch, commander of the *Groupe d'Armées du Nord*, issued N3 its second citation, allowing it to display the *fourregère* of the *Croix de Guerre* on its colours:

'Under the command of commandant Brocard, always ardent, showing exceptional qualities of audacity and skill in combat, particularly formidable towards the enemy. From 19 August to 19 November 1916, it downed 36 enemy aircraft.'

Capitaine Ménard of N26 claimed a 'probable' on 11 December, and the next confirmed victory – a two-seater driven down to crash between Barleux and Belloy at 0925 hrs on the 15th – was scored by Adjutant Joseph-Henri Guiguet. Born 10 March 1891 in Veyrins, Guiguet had enlisted in the army on 10 October 1912 and transferred to the *Service Aeronautique* on 1 January 1913, serving as an observer in MF1.

Entering flight training in February 1915, Guiguet was assigned to N94 and later N95 of the *Camp Retranche de Paris*, and while in the latter home defence unit he took part in a front-wide anti-balloon sweep on 22 May, during which he burned a gasbag at Sivry. Awarded the *Médaille Militaire*, Adjutant Guiguet was transferred to N3 on 16 June 1916, but was severely wounded while attacking another balloon on 1 July. His second victory had come one month and one day since his return to N3.

Wintry weather hobbled activities until 20 December, when GC12 members engaged in 24 combats. Brigadier Adolphe Lemelle of N73 scored his first confirmed victory that day, while Bucquet claimed two probables and Baron of N103 one. The day was marred for N3, however, when it learned that Dorme had been wounded while fighting two Halberstadts over Athies.

Although he was also known as *l'Increvable* ('The Untiring') to his squadronmates, *'Père'* Dorme did not fight with quite the relentless, almost self-destructive zeal that Guynemer displayed. Skilful but calculating, he seemed to believe that vengeance was a dish best served cold, and that the only sacrifice of life should be German. While recovering, he gave his own explanation of what happened:

'I have to say it, I was reckless. Instead of gaining altitude while a distance away, to attack them later, I climbed right at them, right under their eyes, and charged at one while climbing. During that time the other came around and attacked me from the rear. A burst. He missed me. With a vertical bank I turned to face him and swooped down on him. He

Dorme in the cockpit of his Nieuport 17 N1720 *'Père Dorme 3'*. One of the last aces of N3 to use the Nieuport 17 operationally, Dorme's invincible image was shattered on 20 December 1916 when he was severely wounded in the arm during a fight with two Halberstadts (*Greg VanWyndgarden*)

likewise charged me too, and during the pass we sniped at each other at point blank range.'

Dorme was struck by a bullet that left several shards in his right arm, but as the German kept going he turned to pursue him, only to find his engine, which had also been hit, start to misfire. Dorme's wingman, 'Jo' Guiguet, was still below the action, which transpired too quickly for him to intervene, but he escorted the ailing ace back to the field.

Once on the ground, Dorme's wound was judged serious enough for him to be sent to Lariboisière Hospital in Paris, where a month later he was given the temporary commission of sous-lieutenant.

Meanwhile Guiguet, determined to avenge his friend, took off on another patrol that same afternoon, and at 1455 hrs he intercepted an enemy two-seater over Chaulnes. By the time Guiguet broke off his attack, his opponent was going down in a vertical dive, and he later learned that it crashed near the railroad track north of Marchélepot, killing its crew, Vzfw Karl Bücher and Ltn Erich Sauerbray of KG 3.

The next confirmed victories came on 24 December, when Heurtaux downed an aeroplane over Liancourt and Sous-Lt Georges Raymond, another officer of N3 who had scored his first success on 25 September, destroyed an opponent over German lines near Ornes, possibly killing Ltn Lothar Erdmann of *Jasta* 20. Soulier of N26 also claimed an LVG northeast of Cenay-en-Dormois, but it was not confirmed.

Christmas was rendered less merry when Bourdarie succumbed to his wounds, and at 0940 hrs the next day, Heurtaux destroyed an Aviatik north of Bois de Vaux, killing Vzfw Friedrich Rau and Ltn Karl Steinmetz of Fl. Abt. 6. Five minutes later, he and Sous-Lt Guynemer duelled with some Halberstadts, one of which fell to Guynemer east of Misery, while Heurtaux claimed another that went unconfirmed.

There was even less peace over the earth on the 27th, as Guynemer downed a Roland C.II over La Maissonette at 1145 hrs in spite of its observer's fire cutting two of his SPAD's cables, his victims being Vzfw Ernst Dorner and Ltn August Gulting of KG 4. Within the next ten minutes, Lt de la Tour downed a Halberstadt for his eighth victory and Heurtaux sent a Rumpler C I crashing to earth. At 1445 hrs, Sous-Lt Jean Gigodot of N103 scored his second victory between Omiécourt and Fonchette, killing Ltn Albert Holl and Erich Jungmann of Fl. Abt.(A) 287b.

Winter weather prevented GC12 from adding anything more to its tally, but 1916 ended on a happy note as Guynemer, whose score now stood at 25, was promoted to full lieutenant and the group could look back on a very successful first two months, in which its pilots had destroyed 31 enemy aeroplanes for the loss of one pilot killed, two missing, two wounded and two injured in flying accidents.

1917 – GLORY AND DEATH

January 1917 began with the Storks at the top of their game, but the autumn of 1916 had also seen their opponents start to overtake them. Concurrent with the SPAD VII's arrival at the front in late August 1916, Halberstadt D IIs and Albatros D IIs, the latter armed with twin machine guns that nearly tripled the rate of fire that a single synchronised Vickers gun could throw out, were taking the new French fighter's measure.

More important, perhaps, was the legacy of the 40-victory German ace Hptm Oswald Boelcke, who had not only made his squadron, *Jadgstaffel* 2, the scourge of the Somme – and a model for more such fighter units – but had established a sound set of fighter tactics, called the Boelcke Dicta, that would be used to great effect by his disciples after his death in a mid-air collision on 28 October 1916.

Although not the tactical theoretician that Boelcke was, Georges Guynemer was highly influential in persuading Louis Béchereau and the SPAD design team to keep improving what he regarded as a fundamentally sound design so that it could compete with the next generation of German fighters. He advocated twin machine guns and even a cannon-armed fighter, both of which SPAD soon had under development.

By January 1917 Guynemer was flying the new SPAD VII S254, which was powered by the higher-compression 180-hp 8Ab engine developed by Hispano-Suiza. This view also shows his mounting on the cabane struts for an air-to-air camera (*SHAA 92.3739*)

In the meantime, at the end of 1916 Marc Birkigt increased the compression ratio of his Hispano-Suiza motor from 4.7 to 5.3, and the resulting output from 150 to 180 horsepower. The first SPAD VII to be powered by the new 8Ab engine – S254 – had been presented to Guynemer in mid-December 1916. Not only did he go on to score 19 with it, he never had to change its engine – a remarkable indication of both the motor's reliability and of the méchaniciens who maintained it, often joined in their labours by former mechanic Guynemer himself.

Fortunately for posterity, the doubly historic S254 survived combat and decades of retirement, eventually to be restored and displayed at the *Musée de l'Air et l'Espace* at Le Bourget. Other 180-hp SPADs, with improved cooling systems and other refinements, were soon replacing the original versions in GC12's inventory – and allowing the SPAD VII to hold its own practically to the end of the war.

After some days of poor weather, GC12 returned to aerial combat on 5 January 1917, with probables by Guiguet, Ledeuil and Lemelle, but the first confirmed victory of the year was also the first for Lt Marie Henri Joseph Hervet of N103. Guynemer's first claim of the year, on 7 January, went unconfirmed. GC12 would not chalk up another confirmed success until the 23rd, when Guynemer sent a Rumpler C I down in flames over Maurepas, killing Ltn Bernhard Roeder and Otto von Schwanzenbach of Fl. Abt.(A) 216w, and drove down another two-seater near Chaulnes, killing its observer, Hptm Martin Korner of Fl. Abt.(A) 269.

Heurtaux and Guynemer were both credited with double victories on the 24th, the former's including Gftr Franz Budny and Sgt Gottfried Kort of *Schutzstaffel* (protection squadron, or *Schusta*) 13, killed near Parvillers. Just as he was closing in on a Rumpler C I that morning, Guynemer's motor quit, but using what momentum he had, he got in a telling burst and forced the enemy aeroplane down near Goyencourt. After getting his motor working again, he downed a second Rumpler at Molleville farm, killing Gftr Heinrich Bauer and Lftr Anton Haschert, a naval airman attached to Bauer's unidentified *Luftsteitskräfte* unit.

After landing in the ploughed field to examine his kill, Guynemer broke a wheel while trying to take off again, and after ground personnel damaged it further, the SPAD was sent to Paris for extensive repairs. A fifth German went down that day to a foreign 'guest' of N3, Lt Ivan

Lt Ivan Aleksandrovich Orlov (right) and Guynemer stand beside the latter's SPAD S254, the radiator cowl of which shows two bullet holes taken in the course of downing a Rumpler on 24 January 1917. Briefly attached to N3 to catch up on the latest tactics on the Western Front, Orlov scored his fourth victory on the same day, before returning to Russia to achieve acedom, and death (*SHAA B88.473*)

Aleksandrovich Orlov, a nobleman from St Petersburg who had scored his first three victories in Nieuport 11s while leading the Russian 7th Fighter Detachment in Galicia in 1916. Later sent to France to study fighter tactics at N3, he demonstrated what he had learned by scoring his fourth victory. After returning to Russia and rejoining his old unit in March, Orlov became an ace on 21 May, but was killed in action on 4 July 1917.

Cpl Achille Papeil of N3 forced an enemy aeroplane to land and Heurtaux shot another down east of Puzeaux on 25 January, killing Ltn Ewald Erdmann and Günther Kallenback of Fl. Abt.(A) 216. Adjutant André Chainat, back in action after having been wounded on 7 September 1916, claimed an enemy aeroplane on the 25th, as did Alfred Auger, but both pilots were only credited with 'probables'.

Borrowing Bucquet's SPAD on the 26th, Guynemer intercepted an Albatros C VII of Fl. Abt.(A) 266, only to find that his machine gun would not fire. In spite of that, and the 200 rounds loosed at him by the German observer, he managed to bluff the pilot into landing at the aerodrome of Caudron R 4-equipped *escadrille* R209 at Monchy. Guynemer also landed there, and learned from the embarrassed German pilot that the pilot of the Rumpler he had forced down at Goyancourt two days earlier had to have his leg amputated above the knee, and that its observer, Ltn Kurt Just of Fl. Abt.(A) 234, had been killed. That confirmation from a captured enemy brought Guynemer's score up to 30, and added to the legend of a hero who was already the talk of France.

In a subsequent conversation, Guynemer expressed his attitude toward attacking two-seaters. 'It was simply murder for the fast *chasse* aeroplanes to bring down the poor old observation aeroplanes, but in view of the

Adjutant André Julien Chainat in the cockpit of his SPAD VII S117, whose stork and legend *'L'Ouiseau Bleu 6'* were probably applied in blue, as was his personal number '6'. Scoring his 10th and 11th confirmed victories on 2 August 1916, Chainat was wounded on 7 September and transferred to the *3e Group d'Aviation* on 1 January 1917, although he did claim one last 'probable' while flying alongside his old N3 squadronmates on 25 January (*SHAA B76.1365*)

consequences of the observation to artillery and infantry, it was necessary to repress one's natural repugnance to engaging in such unequal combats and to attack the slower aeroplanes with all one's strength.'

Meanwhile, on 23 January N26 had departed Cachy for Manoncourt-en-Vermois in the VIII*e Armée* sector, as GC13 had already done. N3 and N103 made the move on the 29th, followed by N73 the next day. The Germans had recently been bombing the nearby city of Nancy, and the two groups' mission was to prevent further such attacks. After some debilitating early February days Heurtaux claimed an enemy aeroplane on the 4th and d'Harcourt downed two on the 5th, but none were confirmed. Heurtaux had an even busier day on the 6th, damaging three enemy aircraft and sending a fourth crashing in the Bois de Faulz at 1325 hrs for his 20th confirmed victory.

Then, on 8 February, GC12 did what it had come there to do when a force of 15 twin-engined Gothas and seven fighters was reported crossing the lines at Moncel-sur-Seille at 1030 hrs. All the Storks scrambled, but it was Guynemer and Chainat who managed to intercept one of the big aeroplanes. Guynemer attacked from the rear and was met by heavy machine gun fire, but managed to score hits on both of the Gotha's engines. The bomber descended quickly, and soon after Guynemer and Chainat landed, a telephone call confirmed that the Gotha G III had crash-landed at Bouconville, and that its three-man crew, from *Kagohl* 2, had been taken prisoner. The bomber, riddled with 180 hits, was subsequently exhibited at La Place Stanislas Leczinski in Nancy.

Fifteen Germans returned over Nancy the next day, only to lose an Albatros in flames between Tremblecourt and Rogéville, with its pilot, Offsv Richard Krone of KG 2, killed. This was the third victory for Capitaine Alfred Auger.

Born in Constantine on 26 January 1889, Alfred Victor Robert Auger was made a *Chevalier de la Légion d'Honneur* as an infantry officer, before he learned to fly at Pau in February 1915. Wounded on 8 July while flying Caudrons in C11, he requested fighter training the next month. On 22 September he took command of N31, and was promoted to capitaine in December. He shot down an LVG two-seater on 13 March 1916, followed by an Albatros on 2 April, but he was injured in an accident on 16 April. After recovering, Auger was transferred to N3, scoring his success of 9 February 1917 in one of the *escadrille's* remaining Nieuports.

Deullin gained GC12's next confirmed victory on 10 February, a two-seater in flames over Champenoux that resulted in the deaths of Uffz Hermann Heilig and Ltn Otto Michahelles of Fl. Abt.(A) 257. Fair weather on the 14th brought forth 16 patrols, six combats, a probable claim by Bucquet and a two-seater despatched in flames between Custines and Morey by Ledeuil of N103, killing Ltn Max Rolshoven and Wilhelm Sievert of Fl. Abt. 39. Auger was hit in the right side during a fight with four German scouts the next day, but his wound proved to be minor.

On 18 February Brocard was made an *Officier de la Légion d'Honneur* and cited as:

'An elite officer having a high regard of duty besides professional competency beyond compare, and the rare qualities of audacity and composure. As an example, he made the *escadrille* and the *groupe de combat*, which he commanded successfully, into elite units that have been

With four victories to his credit, Sous-Lt Auguste Ledeuil was tantalisingly close to becoming N103's first ace. However, on 3 March 1917 his SPAD VII was brought down by Vzfw Friedrich Altemeier of *Jagdstaffel* (*Jasta*) 24 and he was taken prisoner (*Greg VanWyngarden*)

rendered formidable to the enemy, and have contributed in large part to the success of the Somme operations by ardent pursuit without respite, against enemy aircraft.'

Heurtaux and Guynemer were promoted to capitaines on the same day. On the 22nd Lt Deullin was placed in command of N73, relieving Lt Jean Richard, who was transferred to the GC12 staff.

March 1917 began on a sour note. Dorme, fully recovered and back in action in a new SPAD VII, attacked a Rumpler on the morning of 3 March, but failed to bring it down. On the same day, Lt Robert Richard of N73 was gravely injured in a flying accident in a SPAD VII, and N103's Sous-Lt Auguste Ledeuil, a 29-year-old *Chevalier de la Légion d'Honneur* who stood just one kill short of acedom, became disoriented and came down behind German lines. The Germans credited him to Vzfw Friedrich Altemeier of *Jasta* 24, in spite of Altemeier claiming a Nieuport, whereas Ledeuil had been flying a SPAD VII, which fell into enemy hands intact.

Capitaine Ménard and Adjutant Jeronnez of N26 got GC12's scoring for the month officially under way the next day, with a two-seater downed over the Forêt de Bezange. Capitaine d'Harcourt's aeroplane was riddled with bullets during a tough fight on 9 March, but he managed to bring his fighter in at Lunéville, miraculously unharmed. N103's commander may have been credited to Offsv Anton Dierle of *Jasta* 24 as his first – and as things would subsequently turn out, only – victory.

Guynemer made history again on 16 March by becoming the first Frenchman to shoot down three enemy aeroplanes in one day. His first, in collaboration with Lt Raymond, was an Albatros two-seater in flames between Serres and Courbesseaux at 0908 hrs, killing Uffz August Reichenbach and Oblt Wilfried Buchdracker of Fl. Abt. 12.

Within 22 minutes of that success, N3 engaged Roland D IIs of the recently formed *Jasta* 32 in one of the most inauspicious combat debuts for a German fighter unit. Guynemer brought down one Roland whose wounded pilot, Ltn Rudolf Lothar Arndt *Freiherr* von Hausen, was taken

prisoner. Five minutes later, Deullin sent *Jasta* 32's commander, Oblt Heinrich Schwander, down in flames. Guynemer had a lively discussion with von Hausen in the field hospital near St Nicolas-de-Port after the fight, but the young German later died of complications from bleeding and tetanus on 15 May, and was buried with military honours at Choly, near Toul. Guynemer was up again at 1430 hrs of 16 March, when he downed another Albatros two-seater in flames over Regnéville-en-Haye.

French President Raymond Poincaré had arrived that day to present Guynemer with the Russian Order of St George, 4th Class, but the award ceremony came as an anticlimax after he had witnessed the ace's 'hat trick' from the aerodrome.

The next day saw Capitaines Guynemer and Shigeno team up to send another two-seater down in flames near Attancourt, killing Uffz Karl Mauer and Ltn Eduard von Marcard of Fl. Abt. 12. On the 18th, N26 gave up an experienced pilot, Lt Guy Tourangin, so that he could take command of a newly formed *escadrille*, N89. By the end of the war, Capitaine Tourangin would be a *Chevalier de la Légion d'Honneur* with four victories to his credit.

On 19 March GC12 left the Lorraine sector for Bonnemaison aerodrome, 30 kilometres west-northwest of Reims, in preparation for Général Robert Nivelle's spring offensive.

There was more involved here than just a change of venue, however, for the French were expanding on the local air superiority concept. More *groupes de combat* had been formed, and now GC12 was to be temporarily combined with GC11 (N12, N31, N48 and N57) and GC14 (N75, N80, N83 and N86), along with local army-attached *escadrilles* N76 (*Ve Armée*), N62 (*VIe Armée*) and N69 (*Xe Armée*), under the aegis of the *Groupe des Armées de Réserve* (GAR), led by Commandant Auguste de Reverend. On the 21st, Capitaine Ménard was promoted to command the newly formed GC15 (N37, N38, N78 and N112), and Lt Tenant de la Tour replaced him as commander of N26.

Capitaine Baron Kiyotake Shigeno, a Japanese volunteer in N26, smiles for the camera between two squadronmates. After being made a *Chevalier de la Légion d'Honneur* flying Voisin 3s with VB24 in 1915, Shigeno briefly served in N12 in June 1916 and joined N26 on 17 September. On 17 March 1917 he scored his second confirmed victory in concert with Guynemer (*SHAA B79.795*)

Capitaine Victor Ménard confers with a fellow officer after leaving GC12 to take command of the newly formed GC15 (N37, N38, N78 and N112) on 21 March 1917. Lt Mathieu Tenant de la Tour replaced him as commander of N26 (*SHAA B83.51*)

As the British and French forces prepared for what was hoped to be a coordinated offensive, *'Père'* Dorme officially reopened his account on 25 March by bringing down an AEG C IV northeast of Fismes, where its crew was taken prisoner.

At about that time C46, equipped with twin-engined Caudron R 4s, was temporarily attached to GC12. This was not quite the mismatch it seemed, for although C46's official role was reconnaissance, its pilots, observers and gunners, under the aggressive leadership of 27-year-old Capitaine Didier Lecour-Grandmaison, operated their machines more like three-seat fighters, accounting for 19 enemy aeroplanes – more than a good many single-seat *escadrilles de chasse* – by the time it joined the group.

In April 1917 GC12 was officially given the appellation *'Groupe des Cigognes'*, and N3's Alsacian symbol was adopted for all four of its fighter *escadrilles*. The establishment of a common group insignia meant that those already being used by the other squadrons, such as N26's flaming

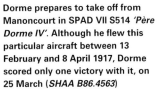

Dorme prepares to take off from Manoncourt in SPAD VII S514 *'Père Dorme IV'*. Although he flew this particular aircraft between 13 February and 8 April 1917, Dorme scored only one victory with it, on 25 March (*SHAA B86.4563*)

torch and N103's red star, would be replaced by storks in different attitudes of flight. Later, some variation was also employed in diagonal fuselage bands for the *escadrilles'* SPAD VIIs, which were blue, white and red for N3, red and white for N26 and N103 and blue and white (the colours of the Virgin Mary) for N73. N103 retained the red Roman numerals by which its individual aircraft were identified, and many of its aircraft had its old emblem – the red star – applied to the upper right wing.

For a few months during the summer of 1917, N3 used green, rather than the more usual red, for the Arabic numbers that identified its individual aircraft. By 1918, however, red numerals, with or without white outlining, were virtually universal for GC12's SPAD XII, XIII and XVII fighters.

Few squadrons associated their pilots with numerals to the degree that N3 did. By the end of 1916, '1' was Brocard's number, '2' adorned nearly all of Guynemer's aircraft, '3' was Deullin's, '6' was Chainat's, '7' was Auger's, '8' was Adjutant Joseph-Henri Guiguet's, '9' was Capitaine Georges Raymond's, '11' was Heurtaux's and '12' was Dorme's. Personal touches included Guynemer's famous legend *'Le Vieux Charles'* beneath his cockpit, as well as Chainat's *'l'Oiseau Bleu'*, Guiguet's *'P'tit Jo'* and Raymond's *'Ma Ninon'*. In addition to his nickname, *'Père'* Dorme's fighters had a green cross of Lorraine on the fuselage upper decking, while one of Auger's later SPAD VIIs (S1416 No 6) had the name *'Je'* and a German being speared on the beak of his stork.

In the spring of 1917 GC12 had the unusual addition of C46, a reconnaissance unit whose Caudron R 4s and Letord 1.A3s were handled like three-seat fighters under the aggressive leadership of Capitaine Didier Lecour-Grandmaison (*SHAA B83.5643*).

Capitaine Didier Lecour-Grandmaison is decorated as a *Chevalier de la Légion d'Honneur*. He and his crewmen accounted for five enemy aircraft, setting the example for several other pilot and gunner aces in C46 (*Jon Guttman*)

Guynemer also applied some creative flair to the sound of his Hispano-Suiza engine. Whenever he returned to the aerodrome after downing an enemy, he would open and close the throttle to produce a humming sound that resembled the words *'J'en ai en'* ('I got one of them').

Ordered to 'blind' the Germans before the Nivelles offensive, Adjutant Jeronnez of N26 burned a balloon at Veslu at 1805 hrs on 6 April. In spite of bad weather the next day, Bucquet of N3 forced a Rumpler C I of *Schusta 7* to land near Hourges, then strafed it until it caught fire. 8 April was Easter Sunday, but it was to be no holiday for airmen – the sky cleared that afternoon, and most of the action that day involved C46. Cpl Damenez's Caudron R 4 was attacked at 1530 hrs and his gunner, MdL Célestin Théron, was fatally struck in the chest, but his observer, Cpl Riviére, saw their assailant go down near Orgeval. Lt Marcel Bloch and Sgts Léon Joussen and Alfred Boyé claimed another enemy aeroplane over Aguilcourt at 1615 hrs, but Joussen was subsequently injured in a hard landing.

At 1600 hrs another Caudron was attacked by four Albatros D IIIs of *Jasta* 19, and although its crew drove one down to land near Orainville, the remaining three Germans shot it down near Viller-Franqueux. The R 4 was credited to the *Staffelführer*, Oblt Erich Hahn. The French observer, Sous-Lt René Wilmes, was mortally wounded in the stomach and the gunner, Adjutant Pierre de Cuypers, badly wounded. The pilot, Sgt Marcel Gendronneau, crash-landed 50 metres from the German trenches and both he and de Cuypers managed to make their way back to the French side of the lines before German shells destroyed their R 4.

It rained for most of 9 April 1917, when the Battle of Arras began, and it snowed the next day. In spite of high winds and clouds on the 11th, GC12 mounted 11 patrols, during which Jéronnez of N26 sent an enemy aeroplane crashing near Cerny-en-Lyonnois, probably wounding Ltn Heinrich Karbe of *Jasta* 22, and Sgt Claude Marcel Haegelen, a 22-year-old former infantryman and F8 member who had been with N103 since 8 March, attacked a balloon at Chavaille and forced the Germans to pull it down.

Its engine ticking over, this SPAD VII of N73 is ready for take-off. It displays placement of the red personal number '8' on the right upper wing, as well as the fuselage side (*SHAA B88.922*)

Sgt Marcel Paris poses in the cockpit of his SPAD VII '7' of N73 in the spring of 1917 (*SHAA B87.179*)

In another engagement that day, Sgt Marcel Paris of N73 claimed a 'probable' but came down wounded, and his squadron mate Adjutant Albert Barioz was killed. They were probably credited to Oblt Rudolf Berthold and Offsv Hüttner of *Jasta* 14. The next day saw an embarrassing loss when MdL Benjamin de Tascher, a 31-year-old Parisian who had flown reconnaissance missions with C30 before joining N26 on 29 November 1916, got lost and landed SPAD S184 at Attigny, behind German lines. He was taken prisoner, but would not remain so for long.

This close-up of Paris in his SPAD reveals his usual legend *'Boule de Neige'* painted beneath the scout's cockpit. During an engagement with *Jasta* 14 on 11 April 1917, Paris damaged a German aeroplane but was wounded in the face and shoulders (*SHAA B87.169*)

Early SPAD VII S172 sports the *'cigogne au style japonais'* of N73 and possibly the number of Lt Albert Deullin, who took command of the *escadrille* on 22 February 1917 (*SHAA B02.946*)

Guynemer was back in action on 13 April, probably downing an Albatros and damaging another, while Soulier damaged a third German aircraft. Guynemer downed an Albatros in flames near La Neuvillette at 1030 hrs the next day, killing Uffz Karl Abelmann and Ltn Heinrich Schönberg of Fl. Abt.(A) 254, and at 1210 hrs the redoubtable C46 team of Lecour-Grandmaison, Adjutant Marie Gaston Vitalis and Sgt Achille Rousseaux sent an Albatros D III flaming down into French lines south of Craonne, killing Ltn Otto Weigel of *Jasta* 14. It was victory number seven for gunner Vitalis, and the fifth for pilot Lecour-Grandmaison and observer Rousseaux. Deullin of N73 drove his 13th victim down in flames near Festieux on the 15th, but SPAD S117 of N3 was brought down by Vfw Julius Buckler of *Jasta* 17 and its pilot, Sgt Achille Louis Papeil, taken prisoner.

Meanwhile, Nivelle's offensive, scheduled for the 14th, still had yet to commence, in spite of entreaties from British Gen Douglas Haig to take some of the pressure off his front to the north. The Canadian Corps had secured Vimy Ridge five days earlier, and the British had made gains elsewhere, but German reinforcements were coming in to stem the potential haemorrhage. Nivelle finally moved on the 16th, launching the Second Battle of the Aisne. French *groupes de combat* were ordered to support the offensive with formations of ten aircraft or more. Brigadier Roger Rigault of N73 downed an opponent in flames north of Cormicy that morning, possibly killing Vfw Rieger of *Jasta* 17.

At 1420 hrs Brigadier Edmond Thomassin of N26 was injured when his Nieuport 24 collided with his opponent, which nevertheless came down in French lines northwest of Guignicourt, where its pilot, Offsv Kern of Fl. Abt. 288, was taken prisoner but the observer, Ltn Walter Utermann, was found dead. Auger, Dorme of N3 and Lutzius of N103 all made claims that could not be confirmed that afternoon, but Rigault destroyed a balloon in flames over Bruyères at 1510 hrs for his second confirmed success in one day.

Dorme took on six Albatros D IIIs west of Orainville on 19 April and sent one of them crashing northeast of Brimont. At first listed as a 'probable', it was confirmed the next day as his 19th victory. His opponents were probably from *Jasta* 31, which lost Ltn Paul Hermann, killed that day. The 20th brought only a casualty for GC12 when Lt Jean Verdié of N73 was wounded.

Cloudy weather held up operations until 1710 hrs on the 22nd, when Deullin attacked what he described as three small two-seaters over Amenaucourt and sent one crashing, killing Flg Albert Karzmarek and Uffz Karl Schilz of *Schusta* 10. Dorme downed a two-seater in French lines near Beaurieux at 1835 hrs that afternoon, its crew being taken prisoner, and at 1710 hrs Auger destroyed another biplane in flames over Lierval, killing Uffz Gustav Richter and Ltn Erich Bersu of Fl. Abt. 212.

Dorme claimed four enemy aeroplanes on the 23rd and two Roland D IIs on the 24th, describing the demise of his second in a letter to his parents: 'I murdered him in cold blood, by surprise, and sent ten rounds into his arse at less than ten metres' distance, under his tail. May the devil take his soul!' Guillaumot and Soulier also claimed 'probables' on the 23rd, while Bucquet forced an enemy machine to land, Adjutant Adrien Fétu of N26 claimed a 'probable' and two others were credited to Caudron crews of R46 on the 24th. The only confirmed *'Cigogne'* victory on either day, however, was scored over Ste Croix on the 24th by Sous-Lt François Marie Noël Battesti, a 26-year-old Corsican who had begun flight training before the war, and had served in *escadrilles* Bl18, Bl3 and C10, before joining N73 on 12 March 1917.

Low clouds prevented further action until 26 April, when two C46 crews brought down enemy aircraft. While returning from a patrol

Sgt René Guillaumot of N3 poses in the cockpit of his SPAD VII '13' *"Ma Renée" (SHAA B91.4643)*

between Coucy-le-Château and Fort Brimont that day, 'Battiste' Battesti noticed his two N73 squadronmates gesticulating wildly, but failed to comprehend what they were trying to say, nor did he grasp the meaning when a two-seater came alongside as he approached Bonnemaison, its observer holding up a wheel. In accordance with what he thought was expected of him, he performed some aerobatics over the field and then brought his plane in for what would have been a perfect landing – had it not been, as he described it, 'a superb nose-over at more than 100 kilometres per hour. I had simply lost upon my departure the right wheel of my SPAD!'

The only other event worth noting on 26 April – and only in retrospect – was the arrival at N103 of a short, 23-year-old farm boy from Saulcy-sur-Meurthe, in the Vosges, who announced his determination to make the Germans pay for their occupation of so much of that region in 1871. That was a common sentiment among Alsatians, and so would be hardly worth further comment, had it not been for the fact that, while flying Caudron G 3s and G4s in C47, the new arrival had already shot down two German aircraft, and had been awarded the *Médaille Militaire* and the British Military Medal. His proven aggressiveness made him a clear choice for transfer to fighters, and indeed GC12's combat reports would soon be making much mention of René Paul Fonck

Dorme downed an Albatros two-seater on 29 April, but C46 lost Letord 1.A3 No 90 and all three of its crewmen, Lt Jules Campion, MdL Marcel

A former Caudron pilot who joined N73 on 12 March 1917, Sous-Lt François Marie Noël Battesti scored his first victory on 24 April, and went on to finish the war with seven – three of which were gained while N73 was attached to GC12 (*Jon Guttman*)

Lamy and Cpl Bosquié, victims of Ltn Walter Böning of *Jasta* 19. Capitaine Shigeno ended 'Bloody April' with an unconfirmed claim, but the French offensive at Chemin des Dames was still under way as May began. Dorme and Guiguet took off at dawn on 1 May, and after an hour's hunting around Berry-au-Bac, they spotted an Albatros two-seater over Montchâlons. After firing several bursts at the intruder they saw it descend out of control, but for want of any witnesses to a crash, it was credited to Dorme only as a 'probable'.

Guynemer had better fortune on 2 May, downing another two-seater and killing Uffz Felix Schilf and Flg Felix Bockenmühl of *Schusta* 10. The next day saw Adjutant-Chef Fonck on patrol with Lt Gigodot when two German aircraft on an artillery range-adjusting mission gave him his first opportunity for combat in his new SPAD. He immediately attacked, firing at both aeroplanes simultaneously, and receiving a good burst in return from one of the German observers, who Fonck said sent some bullets whistling past his ears. 'By a sharp turn, I succeeded in escaping and passed under him,' the Frenchman wrote. 'I then sent a volley of 20 cartridges into him. My satisfaction was great when I saw him fall in a spin north of Berry-au-Bac, but unfortunately, I didn't have the time to verify if he had crashed.'

Among a welter of probable claims, 4 May brought confirmed successes for N3's top-scoring trio. Heurtaux brought down an Albatros whose wounded crewmen, Ltn von der Linde and Wolters of Fl. Abt.(A) 254, were taken prisoner, while Guynemer killed Flg Johann Weidmann and Vfw Walter Lagerhauser of *Schusta* 25. In a letter to his parents that evening, Dorme wrote, 'I caught a Boche who was mocking us over our field, and I simply downed him at Amifontaine. Two pilots of another *escadrille* saw him spin down out of control.' His victims were probably Ltn Kurt Leidreiter and Kurt Böttcher of Fl. Abt.(A) 210.

Adjutant René Fonck had already scored two victories in Caudron G 4s before joining N 103 on 24 April 1917. He is shown in one of the first SPAD VIIs assigned to him upon arrival (*SHAA B87.222*)

During a morning patrol on 5 May, four SPADs of N103 got into a scrap with five German fighters over Laon at 0730 hrs. 'The engagement was an extremely fierce one,' Fonck wrote. 'Quickly we rose from the mist that formed a thick fog and enveloped us. In the midst of it we risked, at any moment, meeting each other in a deadly collision.

'Sgt (Pierre) Schmitter was the first one hit. His aeroplane, riddled in several places, also took a bullet in the motor.

'Sgt Haegelen and Lt Hervet succeeded momentarily in relieving him, but in their turn they were getting the worst of it when I arrived to change the course of events. Twice I attacked the Boches who were machine-gunning my friends. Half-disabled, they had their hands full in the midst of the five enemies who were flying around them. Nothing demoralises a flier like the disabling of a comrade. That day we had further proof of it.

'Despite the skillful manoeuvring that they exhibited, I succeeded in firing at one of the Boches at point-blank range. He had come out of a cloud in front of me. To tell the truth, the opportunity came from heaven. With a well-directed burst, I put an end to his career. His aeroplane immediately nose-dived to a crash at the corner of a wooded area. I followed him in his descent while the other two French "Storks" were pursuing the Fokkers, whose flight was suddenly accelerated as they turned tail and made for home. This victory of mine was not contested. So many witnesses had been present that it was immediately confirmed.'

There is a strong possibility that Fonck's first confirmed victory as a fighter pilot resulted in the death of Offsv Anton Dierle of *Jasta* 24, who may have driven down Fonck's squadron commander, d'Harcourt, almost two months earlier. For all the mastery he demonstrated even this early in his fighting career, Fonck's description also reveals a side of him that was later noted in more ambiguous manner by one of the squadron-mates he had assisted in the course of the action, Claude Haegelen:

'He is not a truthful man. He is a tiresome braggart, and even a bore, but in the air, a slashing rapier, a steel blade tempered with unblemished courage and priceless skill. But afterwards, he can't forget how he rescued you, nor let you forget it. He can almost make you wish he hadn't helped you in the first place.'

This was hardly the most flattering description of Fonck, and it came from one of his best friends! Other pilots, French and foreign, *'Cigognes'* and men from neighbouring groups, would remember him less kindly.

While N103 had had a good morning on 5 May, N3 suffered a grievous casualty that afternoon when Capitaine Heurtaux, whose score then stood at 21, was wounded during a fight with five Albatros D IIIs. Semi-conscious from loss of blood after having been shot through both thighs, his skull creased by a bullet and both cheeks pierced by another, he just managed to crash-land in Allied lines, where he was rushed to a field hospital. Capitaine Auger took temporary command of N3. Heurtaux was probably credited to Ltn Ernst Udet of *Jasta* 15 as his sixth victory.

Dorme also nearly came to grief on 5 May when one of his propeller blades broke, but the mishap caught him at an altitude of 3500 metres, and after switching off his engine, he was able to glide his SPAD safely back to the airfield. It was the turn of Dorme's friend and frequent wingman Guiguet to have the good luck that day, for at 1910 hrs he caught a two-seater between Bruyères and Montchâlon and sent it crashing to earth minutes later for his fourth confirmed victory.

On 6 May Capitaine Jean Jacques Perrin, N26's commander, was transferred as CO to N76. On the 7th, leadership of N26 officially passed to Capitaine de la Tour, who scored his ninth, and final, victory north of Brimont at 0955 hrs that same morning.

On 8 May the Nivelle offensive stalled, to be officially terminated on the 20th. By that time the French had taken 20,000 prisoners and 150 artillery pieces, but they had suffered 118,000 casualties and failed to achieve the decisive breakthrough that Nivelle had promised. Worse, mutinies broke out among the French troops. Nivelle was relieved of his command and his successor, Général Philippe Pétain, quietly restored morale among the ranks. That was achieved not only by shooting some mutineers and containing disclosure of the revolts as much as possible,

Deullin helps start Lt de la Tour's engine for a patrol. On 6 May 1917, de la Tour scored his ninth victory. The following day he left N3 to take command of neighbouring N26 (*SHAA B88.436*)

Ltn Heinrich Gontermann of *Jasta* 15, posing alongside his Albatros D V in the foreground, killed Adjutant Célestin Sanglier of N3 on the morning of 10 May and shot down C46's commander, Capitaine Lecour-Grandmaison, that evening. With his score now at 20, Gontermann was subsequently awarded the *Orden Pour le Mérite* (*Jon Guttman*)

but also by giving the exhausted *poilus* a rest. Fortunately for the Allies, the Germans did not realise the extent of the crisis in time to take advantage of it, but the cancellation of French offensive operations meant that British and Commonwealth forces would have to bear the brunt of fighting for the balance of the year.

Whatever problems the French army was encountering, the *Aviation Militaire* in general, and GC12 in particular, remained committed to keeping matters anything but quiet *over* the Western Front. Dorme scored his 23rd confirmed victory at 1007 hrs on 10 May when he drove an Albatros two-seater down in flames near Sailly en Ostrevent, killing Uffz Max Kandler and Wilhelm Scheffel of *Schutzstaffel* 11. Adjutant Lemelle of N73 also downed an enemy aeroplane between Bievres and Montchâlons that afternoon for his second victory.

Late that morning, however, Adjutant Célestin Eugène Jules Sanglier, a *Médaille Militaire* recipient who had been credited with four victories in N62 before he transferred to N3 in March, was killed north of Berry-au-Bac by *Jasta* 15's commander, Ltn Heinrich Gontermann. The German ace struck again that evening when he sent a Caudron crashing into French lines, killing C46's commander, Capitaine Lecour-Grandmaison, and gunner Cpl Joseph Crozet, although the wounded observer, Sgt Alfred Boyé, miraculously survived. That double blow to GC12 brought Gontermann's score to 20, and soon thereafter he was awarded the *Orden Pour le Mérite*.

Auger became an ace on 11 May when he and Sous-Lt Joseph Marie Xavier de Sevin of N12 brought down a two-seater near Vaully-sur-Aisne. It was the third victory for de Sevin, a 23-year-old St Cyr graduate from Toulouse who would later join the Storks. Deullin downed an Albatros in flames near Loivre that afternoon, and a Rumpler became Fonck's fourth confirmed victim near Aguilcourt. Two days later, Fonck joined the ranks of GC12's aces when he sent a 'Fokker' crashing near Nogent l'Abesse. A two-seater on the 14th brought Soulier's score up to four, and Lt Hervet of N103 scored his second victory over Bouconville.

Joseph Guiguet was given a temporary commission as a sous-lieutenant on 23 May, but later that afternoon his SPAD was fired upon in error by a French 75 mm anti-aircraft gun. A shell splinter severed the control cables to the rudder and elevators and the aeroplane plunged vertically into a grove at Bazoches-sur-Vesles, where the trees slowed its descent somewhat even as it broke up toward the ground. Bonnemaison was only

Lecour-Grandmaison stands before one of the Letord 1.A3s assigned to C46 in the spring of 1917. He was apparently flying one of them when he was shot down on 10 May, although the Germans claimed it as a Caudron. His gunner, Cpl Joseph Crozet, was also killed, but his observer, Sgt Alfred Boyé, miraculously survived (*Jon Guttman*)

Adjutant Joseph Guiguet of N3 poses before his SPAD VII S1105 *'P'tit Jo III'* at Bonnemaison in April. He was flying a new aeroplane – S1418 *'P'tit Jo IV'* – when he scored his fourth victory on 5 May, but was wounded in the leg on the 23rd (*Jon Guttman*)

about seven kilometres away from the crash site, and Dorme, Auger, Bucquet and Guillaumot hastened over to the wreck, where they found Guiguet severely injured but miraculously alive. He was rushed to the hospital at Courville-St Gilles, where the doctors found him to a have suffered several fractures in his skull and face, as well as his right femur.

N3 experienced a day of exceptional triumph and tragedy on 25 May. Guynemer, newly returned from test-flying a new cannon-equipped SPAD XII outside Paris, outdid himself again by being the first French airman to shoot down four German two-seaters, his victims probably including Ltn Georg Feldmann and Georg Oehler of Fl. Abt.(A) 257 over Corbeny, and Ltn Werner Gaedicke, an observer from Fl. Abt.(A) 254, between Guignicourt and Condé. Sous-Lt Henri Rabatel of N.3, who had previously earned the *Médaille Militaire* as a Voisin pilot in VB3 (later

Guynemer returns from a sortie after having scored his 41st victory on 25 May 1917. The day would be spoilt for N3, however, when *'Père Dorme'* failed to return from its patrol (*B88.459*)

VB103) by destroying a kite balloon on 6 February 1916, obtained his first official success in fighters by downing a two-seater near Berrieux. Dorme returned from a morning patrol to tersely note, 'At 0810 hrs, shot down an Albatros two-seater in the woods between Berry and Époye,' but there were not enough witnesses to confirm it.

That afternoon Dorme visited Deullin, and at the latter's invitation he accompanied N73's commander on another patrol. Before the two took off at 1840 hrs, Dorme allegedly remarked, smiling, 'I'm just going to play the soldier-boy and I'll go see Guiguet before dinner.'

Soon after crossing the lines, Deullin reported that the duo encountered a flight of four to six Albatros D IIIs east of Reims. Dorme attacked and may have shot down one of the Germans, but soon after that he and Deullin became separated. Engaging several antagonists of his own, Deullin fought his way clear, and after searching for Dorme, he returned to Bonnemaison, noticing to his dismay the burning wreckage of a SPAD as he made his way back. A few days later, some infantrymen stationed near the Fort de la Pompelle informed Sous-Lt Bucquet that they had seen a SPAD diving 'at full speed' toward the ground about five kilometres from the lines, adding, 'After what seemed like a long time, flames went up from a burning aeroplane.'

Nobody in the group could believe that the 'increvable' 'Père' Dorme could have been lost, but on the 28th Brocard officially announced it. At that time Dorme had 600 flying hours in his *carnet de vol*, and during his 11 months in N3 he had engaged in 120 combats and had 23 confirmed and 29 probable victories.

The answer to the question of which German had the skill or luck to bring down Dorme turned up in a diary entry by Ltn de R Heinrich Claudius Kroll of *Jasta* 9 on 11 June, in which he described the scoring of his fifth victory of 25 May:

'I shot him down near Fort la Pompelle, near Reims. It was a very hot circling fight that started at 5300 metres and lasted down to 800 metres. He suddenly dived vertically and burst into flames when he hit the ground.'

Adjutant Guillaumot and Lt Bozon-Verduraz pose beside the former's SPAD VII S420 (*Louis Risacher album via Jon Guttman*)

Dorme (left) at Bonne Maison beside his last SPAD VII, S392 *'Père Dorme'*, which had the 180-hp Hispano-Suiza 8Ab engine. He first tested it at Le Bourget on 4 April and took possession on the 8th. 'My pressurised aircraft, which is tuned well, gives me absolute confidence,' Dorme said, scoring six victories in it before being killed on 25 May, the fifth victim of Ltn Heinrich Kroll of *Jasta* 9 (*Louis Risacher album via Jon Guttman*)

Dorme's identity was confirmed by means of a watch with the inscription, 'Presented by the Lip factory at Besançon to *Monsieur* René Dorme in remembrance of his heroic achievements during the war', on the cover. Kroll later went on to command Royal Saxon *Jasta* 24, scored 33 victories and was awarded the *Ordre Pour le Mérite,* before suffering a debilitating shoulder wound on 14 August 1918.

Quickly recovering from the shock of losing Dorme, Guynemer sent an Albatros two-seater down to crash west of Condé-sur-Suippes on 26 May, and Soulier claimed a scout and a two-seater, though neither of them could be confirmed. During a patrol between Saint Gobain and Le Fère that day, Deullin and Battesti encountered three Albatros D IIIs at 3700 metres. Although they had several hundred metres' advantage in altitude, two of the Germans, who Battesti thought were 'doubtless young debutantes', descended in the direction of Laon, where he guessed their aerodrome was. The third went straight for Deullin, however, and the two engaged in what Battesti described as, 'a magnificent show of aerobatics in which each showed the other what he knew how to do. The enemy aviator was certainly a big ace to manoeuvre with such precision, and all by himself came to measure up to the fine stork Deullin.'

Throughout the fight Battesti observed from above until he noticed that Deullin had not fired his machine gun once, even when he was momentarily in a favourable position. Concluding that Deullin had either a gun jam or expected him to intervene, 'Battiste' dived into the fray, pulled up in front of the Albatros and opened fire. The German promptly dived away, ending the combat, but upon their return to Bonnemaison, Deullin informed Battesti that at the very moment he had fired, Deullin had placed himself right on the German's tail – and that Battesti's bullet had not only missed the enemy plane, but had narrowly missed hitting his own! 'Battiste' chalked up another lesson on combat judgement from *'Père'* Deullin, relieved to have done so without paying too grievous a price.

On 27 May Soulier scored his fifth victory over a DFW C V, while Sgt Haegelen downed another two-seater for his first confirmed score. On the following day Haegelen teamed up with Sgt Félix Durand of N80 to bring

The day after Dorme's death, Sgt Claude Marcel Haegelen of N103 scored his first confirmed victory, sharing in another two days later. Subsequently serving in SPA100, Haegelen finished the war with 22 victories, including 15 balloons (*SHAA B76.523*)

MdL Auguste Pouchelle was wounded in combat with four Albatros scouts on 31 May 1917. Though he may have been credited to Ltn Josef Veltjens of *Jasta* 14, he managed to bring his SPAD back. On 17 June 1918 Sous-Lt Pouchelle rejoined GC12 as a member of SPA67, serving until the armistice (*SHAA B88.4471*)

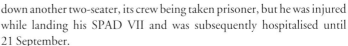

down another two-seater, its crew being taken prisoner, but he was injured while landing his SPAD VII and was subsequently hospitalised until 21 September.

May ended with more casualties for GC12. On the 29th, SPAD VII S265 of N3 came down in German lines and its wounded pilot, Cpl Lucien Perot, became a PoW, credited to Vfw Hans Bowski of *Jasta* 14. MdL Auguste Pouchelle of N26 was wounded in the right thigh during a fight with four German fighters on the 31st, and although he may have been credited to Ltn d R Joseph Veltjens of *Jasta* 14, he managed to bring his shot-up SPAD back.

N26's 19-year-old ace Soulier added a DFW to his tally on 3 June in collaboration with Lt Honoré de Bonald of SPA69 and Sgt Adrien Chapelle of SPA31. Auger of N3 and Deullin of N73 each downed two-seaters on the 4th, but when Guynemer attacked a two-seater over Craonne that day, he had to disengage with damaged controls and a longeron shot through.

The Germans bombed GC12's aerodrome that night, killing two mechanics. Guynemer avenged

them the next afternoon, sending an Albatros down to crash at Loivre, killing Uffz Karl Weingarden and Ltn Franz Wenninger of Fl. Abt.(A) 287, followed by a DFW whose observer, Ltn Hans Philler of Fl. Abt.(A) 267, fell out of the aeroplane and died near Berru. After some bad weather, on 11 June Adjutant Fétu of N26 destroyed a German scout near Laon, and at 0900 hrs the next morning Fonck of N103 sent an Albatros crashing north of Comicy, possibly killing Hptm Eberhard von Seel, commander of *Jasta* 17.

During this period of intense combat, an incident emerged that somewhat contradicted Guynemer's relentlessly murderous image. In his book, *Mein Fliegerleben* (released in English as *Ace of the Iron Cross*), Ernst Udet described how, in June 1917, his unit, *Jasta* 15, was down to four aircraft and its members had to fly lone patrols to cover its assigned sector. During one such sortie near Lierval, Udet noticed a lone SPAD approaching swiftly. 'A loner, like me, up here, looking for prey,' he thought. 'I settle myself into my seat. There's going to be a fight.'

MdL Soulier poses before his SPAD VII of N26. On 27 May 1917, the 19-year-old Soulier became France's youngest ace, and scored his sixth victory on 3 June (*SHAA 87.197*)

The two adversaries came at each other head on, then banked left. 'Then begins the circling,' Udet wrote. 'From below, it might appear as though two large birds of prey were courting one another. But up here it's a game of death. He who gets the enemy at his back first is lost, because the single-seater, with his fixed machine gun, can only shoot straight ahead. His back is defenceless.

'Sometimes we pass so closely I can clearly recognise a narrow, pale face under the leather helmet. On the fuselage, between the wings, there is a word in black letters. As he passes me for the fifth time, so close that his propwash shakes me back and forth, I can make it out. *"Vieux"* it says there – *vieux*, the old one. That's Guynemer's sign.

'Yes, only one man flies like this on our front – Guynemer, who had brought down 30 Germans. Guynemer, who always hunts alone, like all dangerous predators, who swoops out of the sun, downs his opponents in seconds, and disappears. I know it will be a fight where life and death hang in the balance.'

Throughout the engagement Udet, a consummate flier in his own right, was unable to out-manoeuvre Guynemer. 'I try anything I can, tightest banks, turns, side slips, but with lightning speed he anticipates all my moves and reacts at once,' he wrote. 'Slowly I realise his superiority. His aircraft is better, he can do more than I, but I continue to fight. Another curve. For a moment he comes into my sights. I push the button on the stick but the machine gun remains silent – stoppage!'

For what Udet described as the longest eight minutes of his life, he continued his desperate aerobatic struggle, occasionally striving to unjam his weapons. At one point, as Guynemer's SPAD flew over his Albatros, Udet let go of his control column and pounded on the receiver with both fists. Guynemer, who Udet was sure had seen his plight, flew over him again. 'Then it happens,' Udet wrote. 'He sticks out his hand and waves to me, waves lightly, and dives to the west in the direction of his lines.

'I fly home. I'm numb.

'There are people who claim Guynemer had a stoppage himself then,' Udet concluded in retrospect. 'Others claim he feared I might ram him in desperation. But I don't believe any of them. I still believe to this day that a bit of chivalry from the past has continued to survive. For this reason I lay this belated wreath on Guynemer's unknown grave.'

Udet's account, if true, may add to the nobility of the Guynemer legend, but a later, somewhat less idealistic breed of fighter pilot might have pointed out, with the benefit of hindsight, that in this case the French ace's sense of chivalry was somewhat misplaced. Udet, after all, might already have been responsible for wounding Heurtaux – and the total of 62 victories credited to him by the end of the war would include at least one other pilot from SPA3!

On 17 June Sgt Robert Brière of SPA3 scored his first victory, while Lt Gigodot departed N103 to take command of the newly formed N153. Gigodot's score then stood at three, and he would account for one more enemy aeroplane and become a *Chevalier de la Légion d'Honneur* while leading his new command.

In spite of ample aerial activity, the next confirmed success for GC12 did not take place until 28 June, as Capitaine Auger's seventh – a two-seater of KG 2 that he sent crashing west of Pontavert with its crew

Lt Jean Gigodot (right) had scored three victories with N103 when he departed on 17 June 1917 to command the newly formed N153. He would add one more enemy aeroplane to his tally while leading that unit (*SHAA B78.6033*)

wounded. N26 lost its *'Benjamin des As'* the next day when the still-injured Soulier was readmitted to hospital. After his final release on 1 December 1917, he was sent with a military mission to demonstrate combat flying in the United States, and saw no further combat.

Deullin also published a monograph on aerial tactics in June, *Pursuit Work in a Single-Seater*, which would soon be adopted as a training manual by both France and the United States. Among the problems he addressed were the facts that large patrols only served to make the enemy avoid combat in the area, only to return when the patrol had moved on, and that tying a fighter to providing close escort for bombers or reconnaissance aircraft 'paralyses the single-seater and obliges it, often at low altitude, to follow the wake of a comrade who is slow and cannot manoeuvre quickly'.

Following the successful conclusion of the week-long British assault on Messines on 14 June – with little else to show for the spring 1917 offensive – a relative lull fell on and above the Western Front. C46 had ended its affiliation with GC12, and the next success for the group went to Sous-Lt Battesti of N73 on 4 July – a two-seater downed near Berry-au-Bac.

On 5 July Guynemer took possession of a newly arrived fighter that he had requested at the end of 1916 – the SPAD 12Ca.1, or XII, whose

Sous-Lt Benjamin Bozon-Verduraz and Sgt Louis Risacher pose with a SPAD VII of N3 that has had cooling holes drilled in the cowling. Bozon-Verduraz joined the unit on 15 June 1917, followed by Risacher on the 27th, and the two became close friends (*Louis Risacher album via Jon Guttman*)

geared 220-hp Hispano-Suiza 8Cb engine raised the propeller above the cylinder heads, allowing the installation of a cut-down 37 mm Puteaux cannon to fire through a hollow propeller shaft.

Since the cannon's breech protruded between the pilot's legs, the control stick had to be replaced by Deperdussin-type elevator and aileron controls on either side of the pilot – an arrangement that took some getting used to for the average pilot. In addition to the cannon, the SPAD XII had a synchronised 0.30-inch Vickers machine gun that could be used to pinpoint a target, or to help the pilot fight his way out of trouble after the single-shot cannon had been fired.

Anxious to try out his new *'avion magique'*, Guynemer took off in SPAD XII S382 that same day and engaged three DFW C Vs. Not too surprisingly, he experienced trouble with the controls, and the German

SPADs of N3 line up for inspection at Bonnemaison on 5 July 1917. From the foreground, they are S413 '2' of Guynemer, S1329, S1416 '6' of Auger, S1339 '7', Guynemer's SPAD XII S382 (newly delivered with no wings), S1422 '9' of Raymond, S1639 '10' flown by Sous-Lt Henri Rabatel, S424 and S420 '13' flown by Guillaumot (*Louis Risacher album via Jon Guttman*)

gunners forced him to disengage with hits in his engine and radiator. The unhappy ace returned to his airfield to find Général Louis Franchet d'Espérey waiting to present him with the *Rosette d'Officier de la Légion d'Honneur.*

While the SPAD XII had to be taken away for repairs, Guynemer, flying his SPAD VII S413, took on five DFWs on 6 July, and although his machine gun jammed after firing three rounds, they were enough to send one of his opponents down in flames. He also made an unconfirmed claim over Craonne. Tragically, however, Sgt Georges Silberstein, who had just reported to N3 that morning, was killed during a training flight in Auger's SPAD VII S1416, crashing between Chery and Chartreux at 1700 hrs. Sgt René Lecomte of N103 also overturned his aeroplane upon landing after his motor had been disabled in combat.

At 1110 hrs on the 7th, Guynemer shot down an Albatros scout over Villers-Franqueux, killing Ltn Reinhold Oertelt of *Jasta* 19. At 1230 hrs he scored his 48th victory over a DFW of Fl. Abt.(A) 280 over Monssy, its observer, Ltn Walter Gehrs, dying of his wounds the next day. Soon afterward, Guynemer took a few days' leave at home, during which his father suggested that he should retire from combat, at least for a while, since at this point his combat experience might make him more useful as a flying instructor and a technical consultant.

'And it will be said that I have ceased to fight because I have won all the awards,' Georges interjected.

'Let them say it,' his father insisted, 'for when you reappear stronger and more ardent, they will understand. There is a limit to human strength.'

'Yes, a limit! A limit to be passed,' the son replied. 'If one has not given everything, one has given nothing.'

Guynemer returned to N3 determined, in spite of the visible strain that constant flying and fighting had inflicted upon him, to give his last full measure for France.

N3 members look over the line-up at Bonnemaison on 5 July. SPAD VII S420 '13' was regularly flown by Guillaumot, while S1639 '10' was assigned to Sous-Lt Henri Rabatel, who was credited with two victories (*Louis Risacher album via Jon Guttman*)

Visiting Minister of Aviation Jacques Louis Dumesnil congratulates Fonck, whose score stood at six in July 1917. To say that there were more successes to come would prove to be a gross understatement (*Louis Risacher album via Jon Guttman*)

OVER FLANDERS' FIELDS

O n 11 July 1917, GC12 and Capitaine Edouard Duseigneur's GC11 (comprising N12, N31, N48 and N57) were ordered north to aerodromes around Dunkerque to support Général François Anthoine's Ie *Armée,* fighting alongside the British in the Third Battle of Ypres. N3 and N26 were assigned to Briene, N73 to Berques and N103 to Coudekerke.

Operations commenced on 12 July, and MdL Gustave Naudin, a 27-year-old former hussar from Corberon who had been with N26 since 4 February 1917, scored his first victory in concert with a Caudron from C224. During a spotting patrol later that day, he was wounded by a sliver of shrapnel, but completed the mission before returning. The 12th also saw GC12 escort a British bombing raid and Lt Raymond of N3 made a *Chevalier de la Légion d'Honneur.*

On the 13th, a third fighter group in the form of Chef de Bataillon Féquant's GC13 arrived in the sector, with *escadrilles* N15, N65, N84 and N124. Poor weather conditions impeded patrolling until 16 July, when Sous-Lt Rabatel of N3 claimed a probable over the Houthulst Forest.

Shortly after GC12's arrival in the sector, British pilots visited the group in order to familiarise themselves with the aircraft flown by the Frenchmen. During that visit Cpl Louis Risacher, a Parisian-born flying

Sgt Risacher's SPAD VII comes to grief during an attempted forced landing on the beach at Dunkerque (*Louis Risacher album via Jon Guttman*)

instructor who managed to obtain an assignment to N3 on 27 June, recalled an incident that revealed a significant difference in technique between the renowned Guynemer and the rising star Fonck:

'There was a Canadian I remember, one of their aces. I cannot remember his name. He offered to have a mock dogfight with Fonck and Guynemer. Guynemer had the first "fight". It was decided by Guynemer and the Canadian ace that they would cross in the air and the "combat" would begin at once. Immediately, Guynemer was on his tail and he could not get him off. Guynemer had out-manoeuvred a Camel in a SPAD – absolutely!

'Fonck said, "Send me three pilots, and I will attack them. They will never see me". Three English pilots started, and were over the field, where we had lost sight of Fonck. Suddenly, there was a SPAD flying through the three Englishmen. It was Fonck. That was the difference between the two schools. Fonck was a very good pilot, of course, but he never made a dogfighting manoeuvre in the air, he always flew flat. Not to be seen by anybody – that was his style.'

Risacher also noted other aspects of life at GC12. When he first arrived in plain trousers, Commandant Brocard immediately pointed out two airmen to him and said, 'Look here, caporal. See that man with the leather puttees on? It is Capitaine Guynemer, and that one is Capitaine Auger, and they are properly dressed!' Risacher got the message.

Of N3's commander, Risacher noted, 'Auger was a very good pilot and a very good fighter, and had a high sense of what an aviator had to do. That means, after his patrols he would go low over the German trenches and fire his remaining ammunition into them. Guynemer and most of us did this.

'Living conditions were very rough,' he added. 'Brocard used to put us in barracks without comfort, sometimes in tents when other groups were living in châteaux and houses. We were sent wherever there was a French offensive, or where a German attack was expected – we were sent to any hot spot, never knowing what we'd meet in the air. Brocard thought that too much comfort would be bad for us, as he wanted to keep us tough. We had a cook who used to go to town to get food. We ate beefsteak, potatoes and vegetables, and drank wine and water. We had a bar, but used it very little.'

Although French spirits were high, they were entering an extraordinarily dangerous sector. Unlike the *Aviation Militaire*, Britain's Royal Flying Corps (RFC) and Royal Naval Air Service (RNAS) had pursued a policy of constantly sending offensive patrols into enemy territory, whether there was a specific mission to support or not, simply as a gesture to assert aerial supremacy.

The Germans, who referred to their British adversaries as being 'more sporting' than the French, usually responded to the challenge whenever they chose, and on their terms, resulting in the heavy British losses of 'Bloody April', and a concentration over their sector of some of the most battle-seasoned *Jagdstaffeln*. In June 1917 Hptm Manfred *Freiherr* von Richthofen, in emulation of Brocard's GC12, formed *Jasta* 4, 6, 10 and 11 into a permanent 'wing' – *Jagdgeschwader* I – that could be moved to whichever sector needed it to acquire local air superiority.

Unlike the Allies, however, Richthofen did not believe in standing patrols, stating, 'This business of standing sentry duty in the air weakens

SPAD XII S382 was the new fighter armed with a 37 mm Puteaux cannon presented to Capitaine Guynemer at Saint Pol-sur-Mer in July 1917. Promising though it was, the SPAD XII proved to be a handful to fly, though Guynemer used it to score four victories whenever it was not undergoing repair (*SHAA B76.1875*)

Lafayette Flying Corps volunteers Charles John Biddle and Charles Maury Jones undergo training on clipped-wing Blériot *'pingouins'* at Avord. Cpl Biddle joined N73 on 28 July 1917, with Jones following on 15 August (*Jack Eder Collection*)

the pilots' will to fight.' To conserve fuel and time, he would station his *Jagdstaffeln* at airstrips 20 kilometres or less from the trenches, keeping his pilots on constant alert, and letting the Allies come to them. As with the Stork group, Richthofen's JG I, soon to be more popularly known as the Red Baron's 'Flying Circus', had also settled down in Flanders in anticipation of the coming British push.

Guynemer's repaired SPAD *canon*, S382, returned on 20 July. On the 21st Rabatel scored a confirmed victory and Deullin claimed his 17th success northeast of Dixmuide, but on the same day Capitaine Jean Romain Lamon of Deullin's N73 was wounded and brought down in SPAD VII S154. He was probably the second victory for Fw Fritz Schubert of *Jasta* 6, thereby gaining the dubious distinction of being GC12's first member to have a run-in with the 'Circus'. He would not be the last – on 22 July Lt Louis Pandevant of N73 was lost in SPAD S1543, probably the victim of Oblt Kurt von Döring, *Staffelführer* of *Jasta* 4.

On 23 July, N103 got the first of many American volunteers who would enter GC12's ranks through the Lafayette Flying Corps (LFC) – Cpl Leonard Minor Reno. Born in Little Rock, Arkansas, on 23 September 1897, Reno had worked at his father's publishing company in Chicago, Illinois, but after an argument with his parents he left to join the French air service. On the 27th Cpl George Evens Turnure Jr, the 31-year-old son of a banker and stockbroker from Lenox, Massachusetts, also joined N103.

Two more Americans joined N73 the next day. Born in Andalusia, Pennsylvania, in 1890, Charles John Biddle was a graduate of Princeton and Harvard who had left his Philadelphia law practice to enlist in the French Foreign Legion as a means of entering the *Service Aeronautique* on 8 April 1917. Oliver Moulton Chadwick from Lowell, Massachusetts, was another Harvard graduate, and a gifted athlete, who had tried to enlist in the Canadian forces. He had served in a Massachusetts National Guard artillery unit along the Mexican border for two months before enlisting in the French air service on 17 January 1917.

On 27 July Guynemer, accompanying Deullin on a patrol, attacked an Albatros scout between Langemarck and Roulers with his SPAD XII, firing eight machine-gun rounds and one 37 mm shell at 20 metres distance to blow his target apart. His victim was probably Ltn d R Fritz Vossen of *Jasta* 33, who was killed near Moorslede.

GC12 suffered two jolting disasters on 28 July. At 0730 hrs, Capitaine Alfred Auger attacked five enemy fighters over Woesten-Zuideschoote but was shot in the neck, possibly by Vfw Rudolf Francke of *Jasta* 8, who claimed a SPAD over Bixschoote but could not get it confirmed. By sheer will, Auger managed to disengage and reach Allied lines, but died of his wound moments later. Then, during a combat with a two-seater at 0900 hrs, Deullin was struck in the kidneys by two bullets, although he too managed to make Allied lines and was rushed to hospital.

Hastily placed in command of N3 in Auger's stead, Guynemer avenged him that afternoon when he downed a DFW over Westroosebeke using two shells and 30 bullets, although damage from his 50th victim's return fire again consigned his cannon SPAD to the repair shop.

All of these dramatic events had been only a prelude to the Third Battle of Ypres, which commenced on 31 July with an advance by Gen Hubert Gough's Fifth Army over a seven-and-a-half-mile front, with its flanks protected by Gen Sir Herbert Plumer's Second Army on the right and Anthoine's I*er Armée* on the left.

The assault was hindered by the wettest weather Flanders had seen in almost 30 years, as well as the first use of mustard gas by the Germans, who would also introduce the massed use of a specialised two-seater ground attack aeroplane in the form of the relatively small and nimble Halberstadt CL II in September.

By the time the British offensive concluded on 7 December, it would cost the Allies 300,000 casualties.

Amid daily patrolling but little aerial activity, Capitaine Heurtaux reassumed command of N3 on 6 August. GC12's next confirmed victory was scored by Fonck on the 9th – a fighter that he sent down in flames as it tried to attack a Sopwith 1.A2 northwest of Dixmuide. On that same day, however, N26's Japanese member, Capitaine Shigeno, came down

Triumph seldom came without tragedy to GC12. On 28 July Guynemer downed a DFW for his 50th victory, but Deullin was wounded and N3's commander, Capitaine Alfred Auger (seen here), victor over seven enemy aeroplanes, was fatally struck in the neck during a fight with *Jasta* 8 (*Risacher album via Jon Guttman*)

Capitaine Baron Kiyotake Shigeno sits in the cockpit of his SPAD VII of N26 on 27 July 1917. The legend '*Wakadori*,' partly in reference to his deceased wife Wakako ('*dori*' means bird in Japanese), can be seen below the cockpit (*SHAA B93.897*)

This close-up view of Shigeno brings attention to the red number '3' on the upper right wing and a green four-leaf clover on the fuselage upper decking. GC12's Japanese volunteer was wounded on 9 August 1917, possibly the sixth victim of Ltn zur See Gotthard von Sachsenberg of *Marine Feld Jasta* 1 (*SHAA B93.896*)

wounded, possibly credited as the sixth victory for Ltn zur See Gotthard von Sachsenberg of *Marine Feld Jasta* 1.

While recuperating in hospital, Shigeno fell in love with his French nurse. After returning to SPA26, he continued to fly missions, but with less of a death wish – and with the legend *Ninette* under the cockpit of his Spad, in place of *Wakadori*. After the armistice Shigeno married Jeanne and returned to Japan. There, however, his adventures would take a final, ironic twist when he died on 13 October 1924, aged 43, of pneumonia. Unable to live in Japanese society without him, Jeanne Shigeno and their daughter, Ayako, returned to France soon after.

GC13 departed Flanders for the II*er Armée* sector on 11 August, and on the 12th, N3, N26 and N103 moved up to Saint Pol-sur-Mer, outside Dunkerque. Citations and honours caught up with several members at that time, including d'Harcourt, Auger, Deullin, Brocard and Naudin. King Albert of Belgium arrived on the 13th to make Fonck a *Chevalier de la Couronne* and Heurtaux and Guynemer *Chevaliers de l'Ordre de Léopold.*

Another Stork fell victim to the Richthofen 'Circus' on 14 August, when Cpl Chadwick was killed in SPAD S1429 north of Bixshoote at 0945 hrs. He was the fourth victory for Oblt Wilhelm Reinhard of *Jasta* 11, who would ultimately score 20, be awarded the *Orden Pour le Mérite* and be named by Richthofen in what amounted to a will, bequeathing command of JG I to Reinhard in the event of his death.

MdL Lemelle of N73 avenged his American squadronmate that afternoon by dispatching a two-seater in flames east of the Houthulst Forest, and probably downing one of its fighter escorts. His first victim may have been from Royal Württemberg Fl. Abt.(A) 224, which lost observer Ltn Martin Klamroth killed and pilot Ltn d R Oskar Gundermann wounded, while the latter claim may have resulted in Vfw Haass of *Jasta* 29 returning with a serious neck wound.

N73 moved to St Eloi, near Dunkerque, on 15 August, where it received another LFC pilot, Cpl Charles Maury Jones from Red Bank, New Jersey. Guynemer's repaired SPAD XII S382 was also returned to him at this time. In spite of violent winds in the afternoon, GC12 flew 29 patrols on 16 August, during which Lt Raymond of N3 scored his third victory and Fonck of SPA103 downed an Albatros scout in flames, both over the Houthulst Forest. Their successes almost certainly resulted in the deaths of Vfw Walter Hoffmann of *Jasta* 36 and Vfw Anton Shräder of *Jasta* 31.

N3 lost two pilots that day, however – Sous-Lt Rabatel, wounded and forced to land at 0920 hrs by Obflgmstr Kurt Schönfelder, a German naval pilot attached to *Jasta* 7, and Cpl Cornet, who was taken prisoner after being shot down by Offstv Johannes Klein of *Jasta* 18. In addition, MdL Seigneurie of N103 was seriously wounded by anti-aircraft fire and Lemelle of N73 was injured in a crash.

Guynemer scored a double victory in his SPAD XII on the 17th. The first, an Albatros two-seater that he sent crashing near Wladsloo using his machine gun at 0920 hrs, carried Ltn Ernst Schwartz and Oblt Robert Fromm of Fl. Abt.(A) 233 to their deaths. Five minutes later, he used his cannon to destroy a DFW in flames south of Dixmuide, killing Uffz Johann Neuenhoff and Ltn Ulrich von Leyser of Fl. Abt.(A) 40. It was a

While in hospital, Shigeno fell in love with his French nurse and married her. He is shown here after the war with his daughter, Ayako. Easily Japan's most experienced combat pilot, Shigeno died of pneumonia on 13 October 1924, aged 42. Unable to cope in Japanese society alone, Jeanne Shigeno returned to France with Ayako soon after (*SHAA B77.1460*)

Another GC12 loss in August was Sous-Lt Henri Rabatel of N3, who was wounded and his SPAD VII S1639 brought down by Obflgmstr Kurt Schönfelder, a German naval pilot attached to *Jasta* 7 (*Greg VanWyngarden*)

less auspicious day for N103's Cpl Turnure, who was injured when he cracked up in SPAD S1637 at Furnes.

Sgt Jean Hénin of N3 downed an enemy aeroplane in flames at 0745 hrs on 18 August, while Guynemer claimed a 'probable' over an aggressively crewed two-seater that put his SPAD XII temporarily out of action once more. At 1020 hrs that morning N73's Cpl Julian Cornell Biddle (a cousin of American ace Charles Biddle) from Philadelphia took off on a training flight, only to crash in the sea off Dunkerque. Only parts of his SPAD VII – S1300 – were recovered. He had been with the *escadrille* for just a week.

In a letter home on 21 August, Charles Biddle wrote:

'My friend Oliver Chadwick was killed by the Boche on Tuesday. He sailed in to help out another machine that was being attacked and was in turn attacked from the rear by two other machines. At least this is what happened as far as we can learn.

'Then on the 18th Julian was killed, so it was a very bad week for the Americans here. I am terribly sorry about Julian, and I naturally feel his loss very keenly for we were always very good friends and had had a lot of fun together since coming to France. He was an excellent pilot in the schools and extremely conscientious and hard working. He got his military license in a remarkably short time and sailed through all the tests without the slightest mishap. Once he had had time to gain a little experience here at the front I feel sure that he would have done very well. Julian and Oliver and I might have had some great Boche hunting expeditions together if luck had not broken so against them. I am glad to say that Maury Jones arrived here the day after Oliver was lost, so I am not left the only American in the escadrille.'

In spite of the SPAD XII's mixed fortunes, Guynemer's successes in it encouraged the *Aviation Militaire* to order 1000 cannon fighters, though it is doubtful that more than 20 were completed. Greater priority was placed on the more conventional SPAD XIII, with its twin Vickers machine guns. In any case, the SPAD XII was a handful for all but the most skilled pilots, and in the months that followed the few cannon SPADs that reached the front would generally be flown by aces, including at least one other in GC12.

The SPAD13.C1 or XIII was, like the XII, designed around Marc Birkigt's new 220-hp Hispano-Suiza 8B engine, which used a spur reduction gear to transfer that power to the propeller. The first SPAD XIIIs had been ordered into production in February 1917, Sous-Lt

This line-up of N73 SPAD VIIs apparently includes S1300 at left. On 18 August 1917 that aircraft inexplicably crashed in the sea off Dunkerque, killing its pilot, Cpl Julian Biddle, Lafayette Flying Corps volunteer and cousin of N73's Cpl Charles Biddle (*SHAA B88.1127*)

Lt Deullin dons his flying clothes for a sortie in his early-model SPAD XII S501 (*SHAA B91.5584*)

Deullin (centre) takes possession of a somewhat less welcome addition to the SPA73 inventory – a SPAD XI two-seater for reconnaissance missions (*SHAA B92.26*)

Dorme having test-flown one at Buc on 4 April 1917. At least one other SPAD XIII underwent frontline evaluation on 26 April. By the end of August Guynemer, who had so strongly advocated more power, speed and armament for the basic SPAD VII, had received new SPAD XIII S504.

Fonck downed an Albatros two-seater on 19 August and sent another down in flames west of Ypres on the 20th, while Guynemer used his new SPAD XIII to obtain his 53rd victory at the expense of a DFW near Poperinghe. Guynemer's score was now second only to Richthofen's 61, and to cap off the day, RFC Maj Gen Hugh Trenchard visited St Pol to present Guynemer with the Distinguished Service Order.

The 21st saw Fonck shoot down a two-seater over Dixmuide, but Lt Paul Dumas of N103 and Sous-Lt André Dezarrois of N26 were wounded. On 22 August Fonck sent a two-seater down in flames east of Ypres for his 11th victory – and his fourth in as many days. It was also GC12's last confirmed success for the month.

September began well as Deullin returned to command N73, and to find new SPAD XIII S501 waiting for him. On the evening of the 3rd, however, Heurtaux took off to test-fly a new SPAD XIII and, seeing an enemy aeroplane below him as he approached Ypres, he dived to attack. Heurtaux suffered a gun jam, however, and as he broke away, the German – possibly Ltn Otto Kunst of *Jasta 7*, whose claim that day was not confirmed – punctured his oil line and put several bullets through his femoral artery.

Photographed during a ceremony at GC12, Capitaine Heurtaux hobbles on two canes, lending mute testimony to the seriousness of the leg wound he sustained on 2 September 1917 (*Greg VanWyngarden*)

Heurtaux would have bled to death in the air, but the incendiary bullet that passed through his thigh cauterised the wound, permitting him to reach British lines near Pervyse. That injury put him out of the war, however, save to lecture on combat tactics in the United States. As it was, Alfred Heurtaux had 21 victories, for which he had been made a *Chevalier de la Légion d'Honneur* and received the *Croix de Guerre* with 15 palms and two bronze stars.

Sgt André Pernelle of N103 downed an enemy aeroplane northeast of Ypres on 9 September, but Adjutant Pierre Petit-Darriel of N3 was wounded in combat. Thus far, GC12's fortunes over Flanders had been mixed at best, but its most grievous loss was yet to come.

Guynemer had gone on leave on 24 August, but typically had spent much of it visiting the SPAD representative at Buc, making further suggestions to improve its fighters. Much of the French public's adulation of Guynemer stemmed from his relentless patriotism, but anyone who compared a photograph of him in 1916 with one taken of him in the summer of 1917 could see just how much of a toll that incessant combat activity had taken on him.

After Guynemer returned to St Pol, bad weather grounded him until 10 September, and in the course of that sortie a malfunctioning water pump control forced him to land his SPAD XIII at the Belgian airfield of Les Moeures. While waiting for his own aeroplane to be repaired, Guynemer borrowed Deullin's SPAD to attack a large number of German aircraft spotted nearby, only to be struck by four bullets and compelled to land. Soon after taking off in yet another SPAD, a loose carburettor cover resulted in fuel overflow and the engine caught fire, again forcing him to land.

SPA3 suffered another loss on 10 September when Adjutant Pierre Petit-Darriel was wounded in action – but worse fortune was to befall the *escadrille* the following day (*SHAA B82.743*)

Visibly exasperated, Guynemer ordered his mechanics to have S504 ready to fly at 0800 hrs the next morning, but fog delayed take-off until 0825 hrs. Sous-Lt Jean Seraphin Benjamin Emmaneul Bozon-Verduraz and Sgt Risacher were slated to accompany him, but the latter's engine would not start and Guynemer impatiently took off with Bozon-Verduraz only.

At an altitude of 5000 ft, the morning haze dissipated and at 12,000 ft the Frenchmen spotted a DFW C V northeast of Ypres, which they attacked from above and behind. Bozon-Verduraz missed and had pulled up to prepare for another diving pass when he noticed eight enemy aircraft approaching and turned toward them. The Germans turned away, so Bozon-Verduraz went back to find Guynemer, only to see no trace of him or the DFW. Risacher, who took off belatedly, later described what he saw:

A new SPAD XIII with twin Vickers guns, S504 acquired the SPA3 livery and '2' of Capitaine Guynemer. On 20 August he used it to bring down a DFW C V for his 53rd victory, little suspecting that that would also be his last (*SHAA B97.1685*)

An exasperated Capitaine Guynemer boards his SPAD XIII after repairs at Les Moeures on 10 September. The next day he took off in S504, accompanied by Bozon-Verduraz. Only the latter returned (*Greg VanWyngarden*)

'On 11 September 1917, Guynemer was flying with Bozone-Verduraz. I myself was asked to fly much lower. I was pleased with it – when you fly lower, you are the ham to attract the attacker. I came. We had many fights. I was alone with a young pilot. I saw Guynemer for a moment over the Houthulst Forest, 30 miles from Nieuport. Guynemer was very high, and I saw his aeroplane come down in a spin. So I came inside my lines to see what was going to happen.

'I recognised Guynemer's SPAD because his aeroplane had pocket extensions on the lower wing, so instead of being round it was square. He was the first in the squadron to have that.

'Suddenly, I saw him stop his vrille and dive. I believed that he was going to attack another German aeroplane, so I returned to my Pfalz. That's what occurred, that's what I saw. Guynemer mis-attacked a German aeroplane, missed him, and at that moment Bozon-Verduraz, instead of going on to attack the same plane, left Guynemer because he saw five or six German scouts coming to save the two-seater Guynemer was attacking.

'So Bozon-Verduraz climbed, facing the scouts, to permit Guynemer to try another attack. But unfortunately Guynemer thought he was attacking a single-seater. In fact, it was a new aeroplane, very small, but a two-seater with a machine-gun behind. He was shot by the gunner and received a wound in the throat. He fell back, then fell forward, and his aeroplane fell into a spin. As his legs straightened, the aeroplane did too.'

Upon returning to St Pol-sur-Mer at 1020 hrs, Bozon-Verduraz's first words were, 'Has he landed yet?' 'We expected Guynemer for a while,' Risacher recalled, 'and we phoned everywhere to get news of him, and we got an answer from the English. They said a SPAD had landed between the lines. The pilot jumped out of the aeroplane and he was in an artillery truck. Very sportingly the English said their infantry were going to attack to save Guynemer. And they did. But it wasn't Guynemer. It was a Canadian pilot who was flying the SPAD, and he was rescued. We heard no more news about Guynemer for a few days.'

Capitaine Guynemer prepares for take-off in his SPAD XIII S504 in September 1917. Note the dark (black?) 'X' on the upper wing centre section (*SHAA B97.1684*)

One month later, the Germans announced that Ltn Kurt Wissemann of *Jasta* 3 had killed Guynemer for his fifth victory. A sergeant of the German 413th Regiment certified that he had witnessed the SPAD's crash, and identified the body, noting that Guynemer had died of a head wound, one of his fingers had been shot off and a leg was broken. An Allied artillery barrage drove the Germans back before they could properly bury the body, which thus vanished amid the chaos that was the Western Front.

Although Wissemann has come to traditionally retain the credit for Guynemer's demise, that is eternally contradicted by the testimonies of both Bozon-Verduraz and Risacher, which state that he was last seen engaging a two-seater. Could Wissemann have intervened unnoticed, or shot at the SPAD over Poelkapelle and, seeing it go down to the observer of the two-seater he was aiding, assume that it was his fire that brought it down? Although Wissemann claimed a SPAD over the right location, he never claimed that it was Guynemer's.

By the time the *Luftsteitskräfte* made its pronouncement, Wissemann was no longer available for comment, having been killed on 28 September by two SE 5as of No 56 Sqn, RFC, flown by Capt Geoffrey H Bowman and Lt Reginald T C Hodge.

Another possibility is that the two-seater that shot Guynemer down never returned to put in the claim. The most likely candidate is Rumpler C IV 1463/17 from Fl. Abt.(A) 224w, crewed by Flg Georg Seibert and Ltn d R Max Psaar, which was shot down near Oudekapelle, 17 kilometres north of Poelkapelle, by Lt Maurice Medaets of the Belgian Air Service.

Whatever the tragic circumstances of his death, Georges Guynemer went into French legend as its second-ranking ace who, a popular children's myth insisted, had flown so high he could never come down. At neighbouring N73, however, Charles Biddle combined his expression of grief with a prescient appraisal of the great ace's condition at the time:

'I believe his health was very far from good, and high altitudes sometimes made him so sick he had to come down. He would fly for a week and then go away for a rest, as he was not strong enough to stand any more. In the course of several hundred flights he had been shot down seven times and twice wounded. To keep at it under such circumstances, and after all he had gone through, a man's heart has to be in the right place, and no mistake. He certainly deserved to live the rest of his days in peace, and one hates to see a man like that get it.

'The evening before he disappeared, I was standing on the field when he landed with a dead motor caused by a bullet in it. There were three others through his wings. He had attacked another two-seater, something went wrong with his motor at the crucial moment and this gave the Boche a good shot and spoiled his own chance of bringing down his opponent. A little episode like that rolled off his back like water off a duck, perhaps a little too easily I fear. Long immunity breeds a contempt of danger which is probably the greatest danger of all. Guynemer's loss naturally throws more or less of a gloom over everyone.'

'The Storks' reaction to the news of Guynemer's death was that we would fly more and more to avenge him,' declared Risacher. 'We would kill every German we could. Bozon-Verduraz and myself, despite the disappearance of Guynemer, wanted to see that the Storks had the same

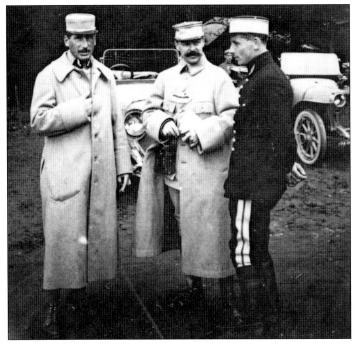

Capitaine Henri Jacques Jean Horment, seen at left with Lt Voisin and Capitaine Alfred Heurtaux, took command of GC12 on 30 September 1917 following Brocard's promotion to *Chef-de-Cabinet du Sous-secrétaire d'État à l'Aéronautique* in Paris. Horment, who had been twice wounded and made a *Chevalier de la Légion d'Honneur* for his leadership of N62, was replaced as GC12's commander by Capitaine Charles Dupuy on 4 May 1918 (*SHAA B84.2113*)

successes as when he was alive.' The cumulative loss of Guynemer, Heurtaux, Auger and Dorme must have had a negative psychological impact on N3, however, for the *escadrille* only scored two victories for the rest of 1917.

On the administrative level, Lt Gustave Lagache took acting charge of N3 until 16 September, when Lt Georges Raymond was officially given command. By that time the last of the original *Escadrille des Cigognes'* Nieuports had been withdrawn, and it was officially redesignated SPA3.

At neighbouring N103, René Fonck also swore to avenge Guynemer, and on 14 September he destroyed a two-seater in flames over Poelcapelle. 'Such was the funeral of Guynemer to me,' he later wrote. As he approached GC12's aerodrome, Fonck announced his 12th victory by manipulating the throttle to produce the *'J'en ai en'* sound that had been the late Guynemer's signature. Whatever his intent, his fellow Storks viewed it resentfully as a tactless act, and some reproached him for it to his face. Fonck did not reply to his detractors. 'It is not part of my makeup to emulate the deeds of others,' he wrote.

Although his combination of aloofness and self-aggrandising manner made him unpopular among fellow Storks, Fonck's personal regimen between missions was more mature than Guynemer's. Rather than burn himself out with constant combat, he would rest regularly between missions, and spend the down time that others might spend at the bar practicing his marksmanship. The results would manifest themselves in the following year, in which Fonck became GC12's deadliest hunter.

Sgt Roger Tassou of N73 (left) and Adjutant Pierre Petit-Darriel of SPA3 clown around for the camera. On 27 September 1917 Tassou was put under 30 days house arrest for flying low over the beach and causing a severe accident. On 6 November, however, he was cited for valour in combat, and on 25 January 1918 he was promoted to adjutant (*Louis Risacher album via Jon Guttman*)

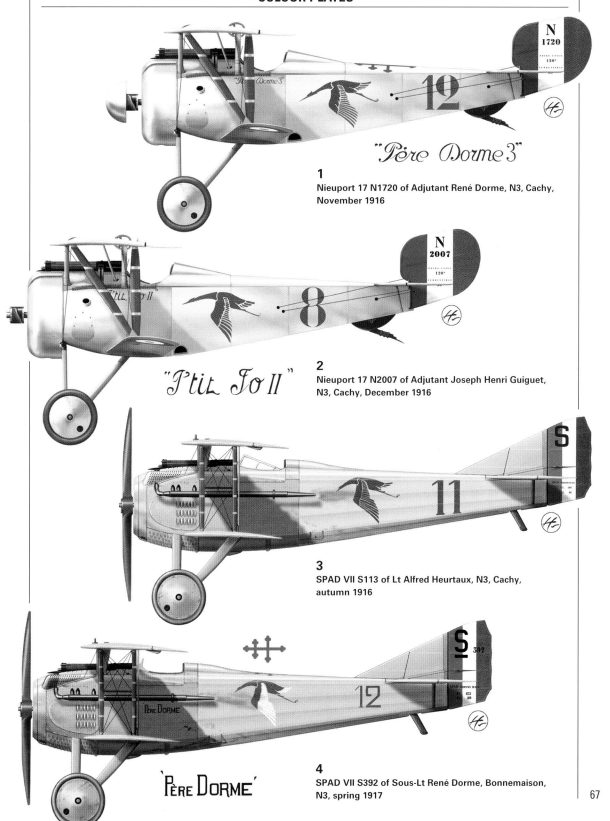

"Père Dorme 3"

1
Nieuport 17 N1720 of Adjutant René Dorme, N3, Cachy,
November 1916

"P'tit Jo II"

2
Nieuport 17 N2007 of Adjutant Joseph Henri Guiguet,
N3, Cachy, December 1916

3
SPAD VII S113 of Lt Alfred Heurtaux, N3, Cachy,
autumn 1916

`Père Dorme´

4
SPAD VII S392 of Sous-Lt René Dorme, Bonnemaison,
N3, spring 1917

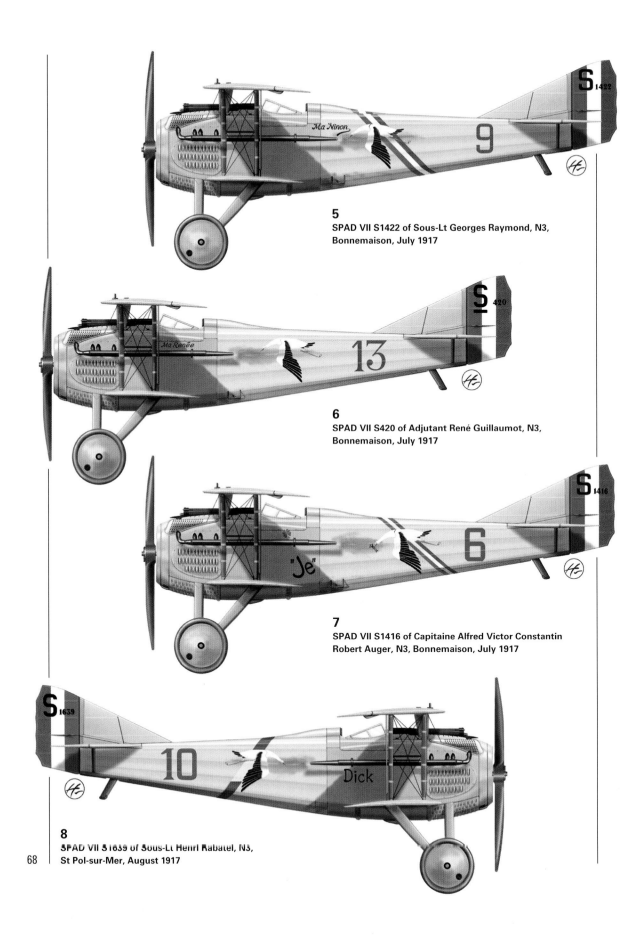

5
SPAD VII S1422 of Sous-Lt Georges Raymond, N3,
Bonnemaison, July 1917

6
SPAD VII S420 of Adjutant René Guillaumot, N3,
Bonnemaison, July 1917

7
SPAD VII S1416 of Capitaine Alfred Victor Constantin
Robert Auger, N3, Bonnemaison, July 1917

8
SPAD VII S1639 of Sous-Lt Henri Rabatel, N3,
St Pol-sur-Mer, August 1917

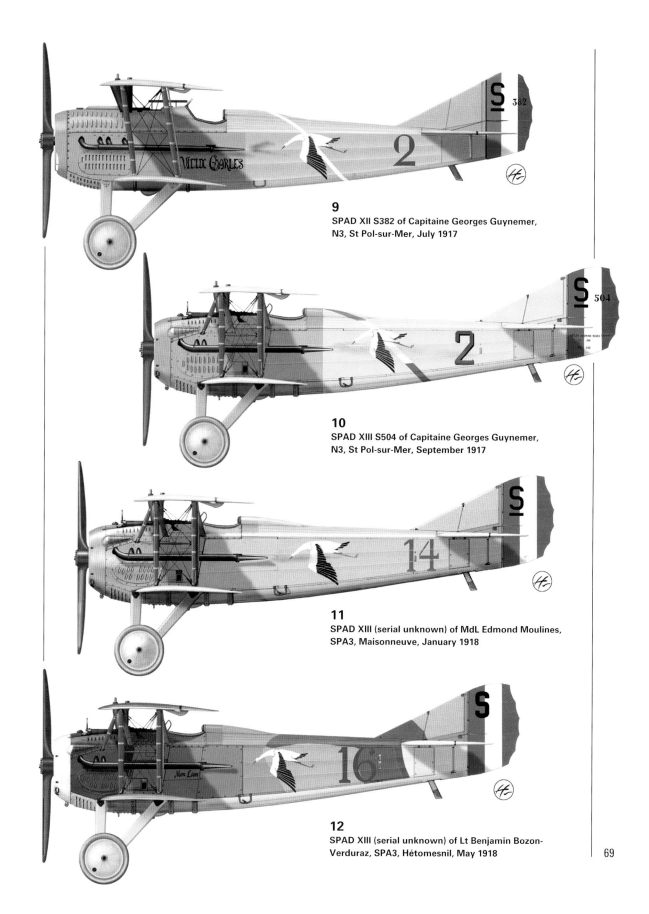

9
SPAD XII S382 of Capitaine Georges Guynemer,
N3, St Pol-sur-Mer, July 1917

10
SPAD XIII S504 of Capitaine Georges Guynemer,
N3, St Pol-sur-Mer, September 1917

11
SPAD XIII (serial unknown) of MdL Edmond Moulines,
SPA3, Maisonneuve, January 1918

12
SPAD XIII (serial unknown) of Lt Benjamin Bozon-
Verduraz, SPA3, Hétomesnil, May 1918

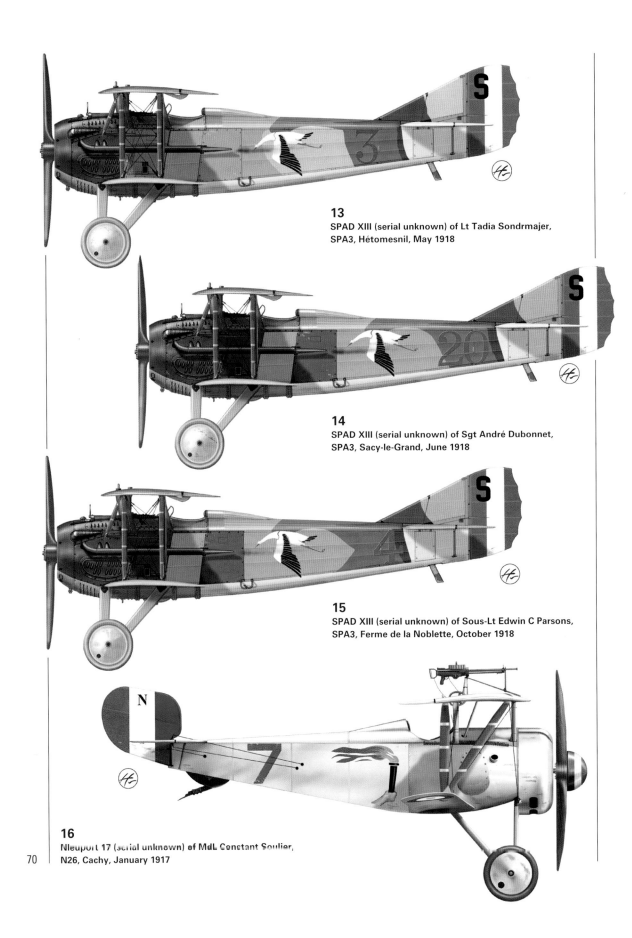

13
SPAD XIII (serial unknown) of Lt Tadia Sondrmajer,
SPA3, Hétomesnil, May 1918

14
SPAD XIII (serial unknown) of Sgt André Dubonnet,
SPA3, Sacy-le-Grand, June 1918

15
SPAD XIII (serial unknown) of Sous-Lt Edwin C Parsons,
SPA3, Ferme de la Noblette, October 1918

16
Nieuport 17 (serial unknown) of MdL Constant Soulier,
N26, Cachy, January 1917

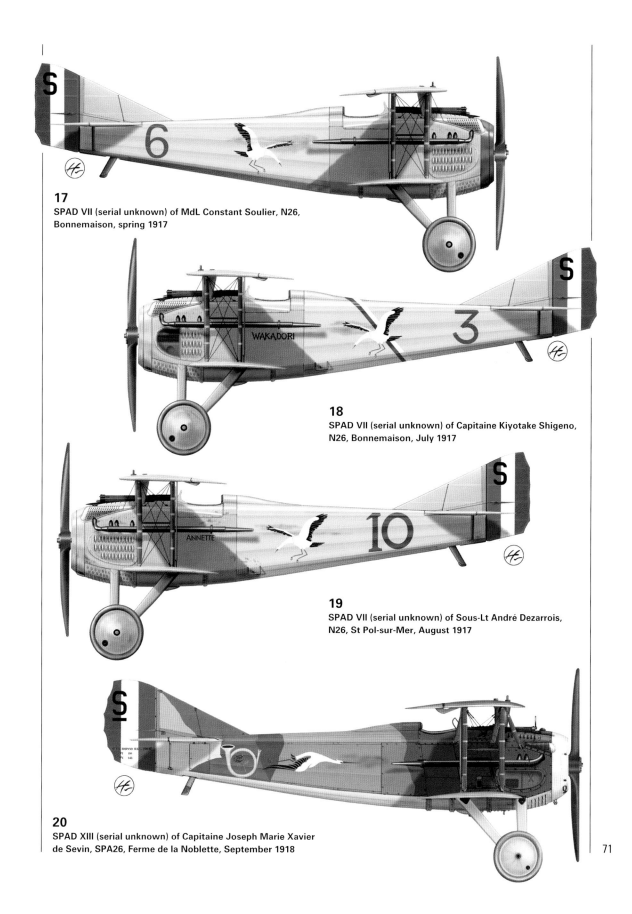

17
SPAD VII (serial unknown) of MdL Constant Soulier, N26,
Bonnemaison, spring 1917

18
SPAD VII (serial unknown) of Capitaine Kiyotake Shigeno,
N26, Bonnemaison, July 1917

19
SPAD VII (serial unknown) of Sous-Lt André Dezarrois,
N26, St Pol-sur-Mer, August 1917

20
SPAD XIII (serial unknown) of Capitaine Joseph Marie Xavier
de Sevin, SPA26, Ferme de la Noblette, September 1918

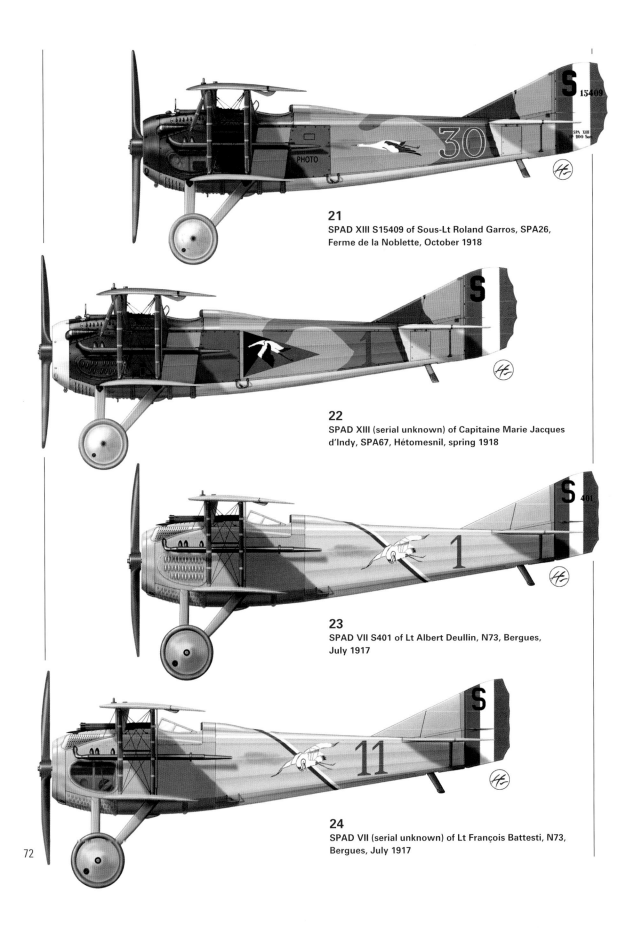

21
SPAD XIII S15409 of Sous-Lt Roland Garros, SPA26,
Ferme de la Noblette, October 1918

22
SPAD XIII (serial unknown) of Capitaine Marie Jacques
d'Indy, SPA67, Hétomesnil, spring 1918

23
SPAD VII S401 of Lt Albert Deullin, N73, Bergues,
July 1917

24
SPAD VII (serial unknown) of Lt François Battesti, N73,
Bergues, July 1917

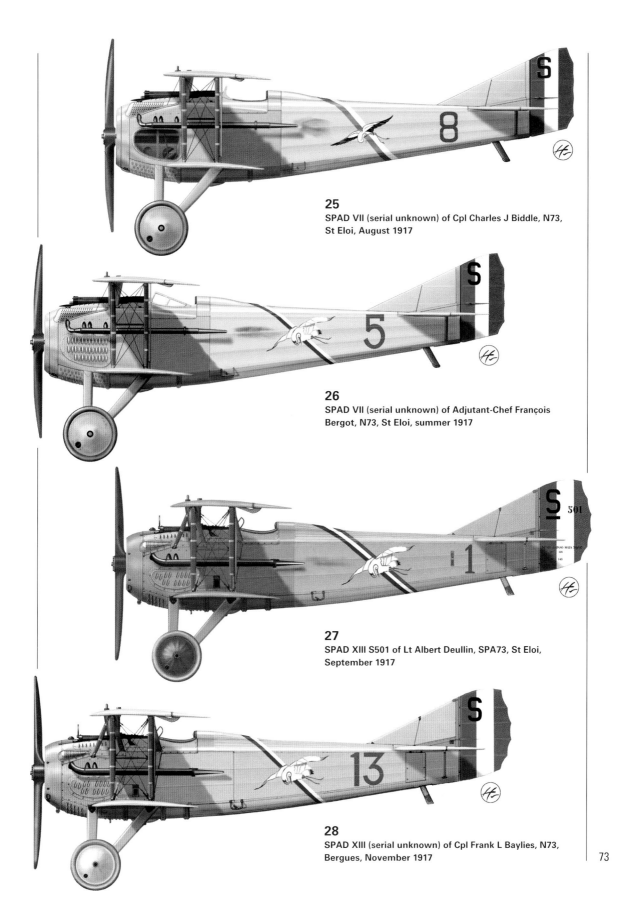

25
SPAD VII (serial unknown) of Cpl Charles J Biddle, N73,
St Eloi, August 1917

26
SPAD VII (serial unknown) of Adjutant-Chef François
Bergot, N73, St Eloi, summer 1917

27
SPAD XIII S501 of Lt Albert Deullin, SPA73, St Eloi,
September 1917

28
SPAD XIII (serial unknown) of Cpl Frank L Baylies, N73,
Bergues, November 1917

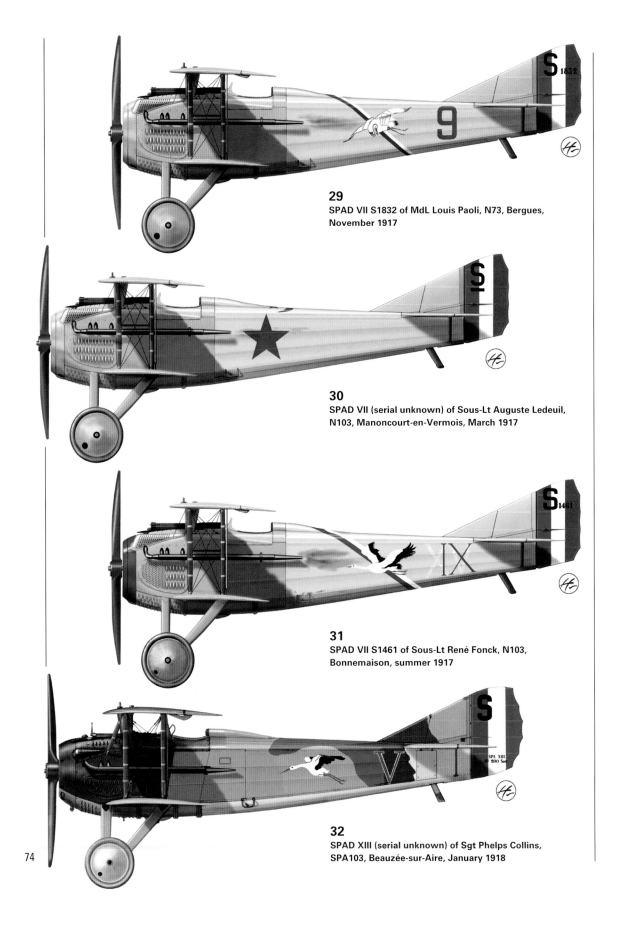

29
SPAD VII S1832 of MdL Louis Paoli, N73, Bergues,
November 1917

30
SPAD VII (serial unknown) of Sous-Lt Auguste Ledeuil,
N103, Manoncourt-en-Vermois, March 1917

31
SPAD VII S1461 of Sous-Lt René Fonck, N103,
Bonnemaison, summer 1917

32
SPAD XIII (serial unknown) of Sgt Phelps Collins,
SPA103, Beauzée-sur-Aire, January 1918

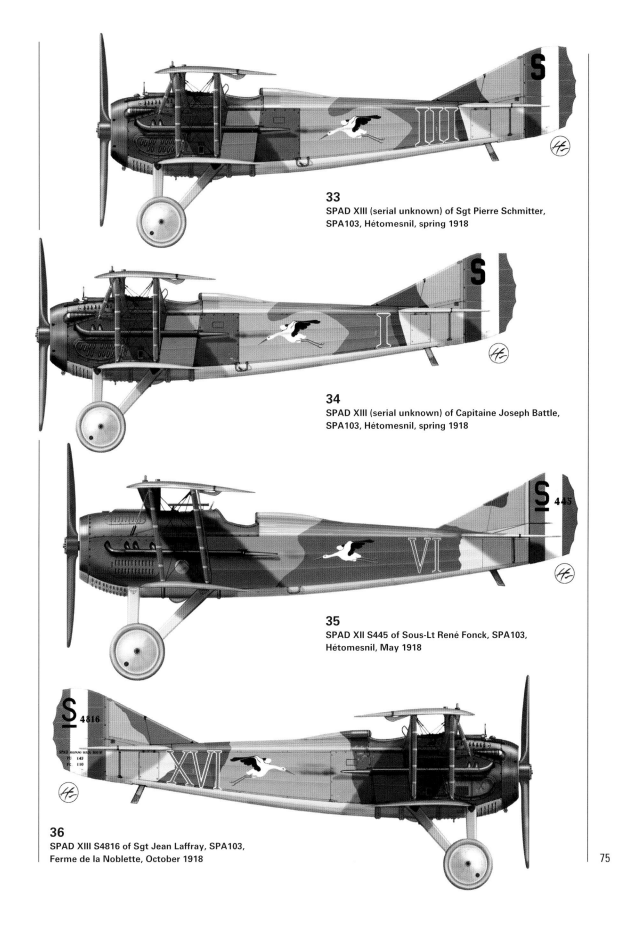

33
SPAD XIII (serial unknown) of Sgt Pierre Schmitter,
SPA103, Hétomesnil, spring 1918

34
SPAD XIII (serial unknown) of Capitaine Joseph Battle,
SPA103, Hétomesnil, spring 1918

35
SPAD XII S445 of Sous-Lt René Fonck, SPA103,
Hétomesnil, May 1918

36
SPAD XIII S4816 of Sgt Jean Laffray, SPA103,
Ferme de la Noblette, October 1918

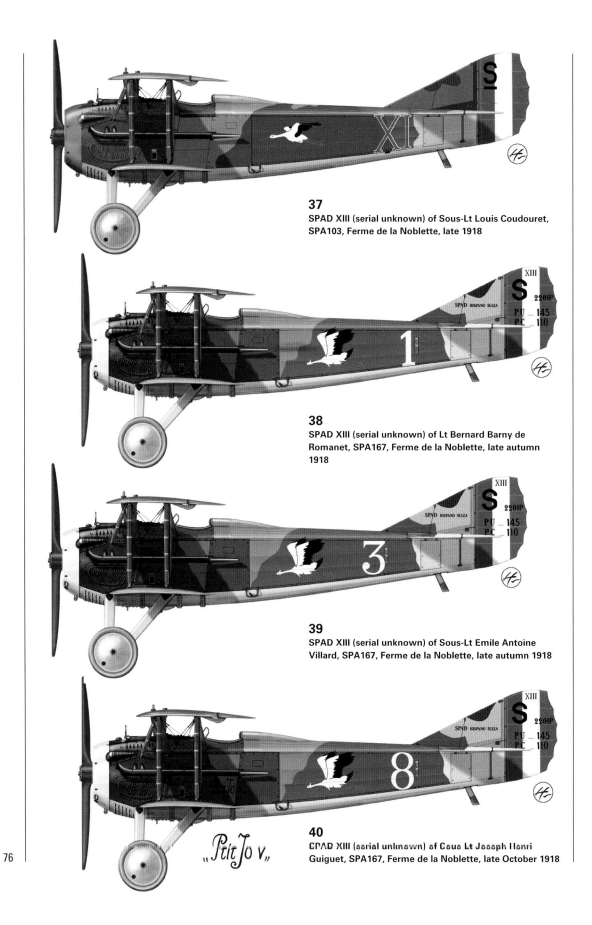

37
SPAD XIII (serial unknown) of Sous-Lt Louis Coudouret,
SPA103, Ferme de la Noblette, late 1918

38
SPAD XIII (serial unknown) of Lt Bernard Barny de
Romanet, SPA167, Ferme de la Noblette, late autumn
1918

39
SPAD XIII (serial unknown) of Sous-Lt Emile Antoine
Villard, SPA167, Ferme de la Noblette, late autumn 1918

40
SPAD XIII (serial unknown) of Sous-Lt Joseph Henri
Guiguet, SPA167, Ferme de la Noblette, late October 1918

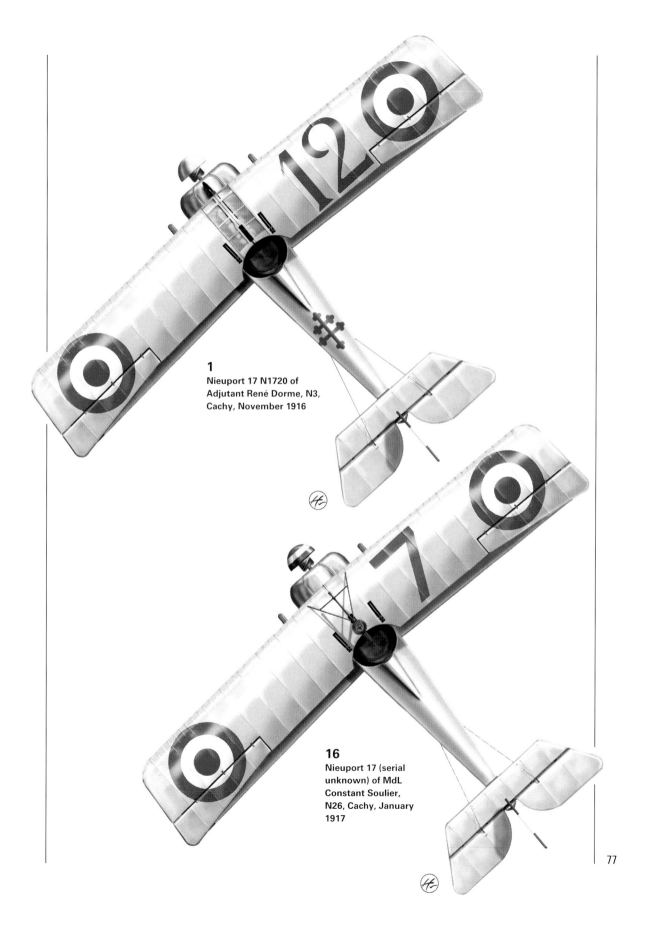

1
Nieuport 17 N1720 of
Adjutant René Dorme, N3,
Cachy, November 1916

16
Nieuport 17 (serial
unknown) of MdL
Constant Soulier,
N26, Cachy, January
1917

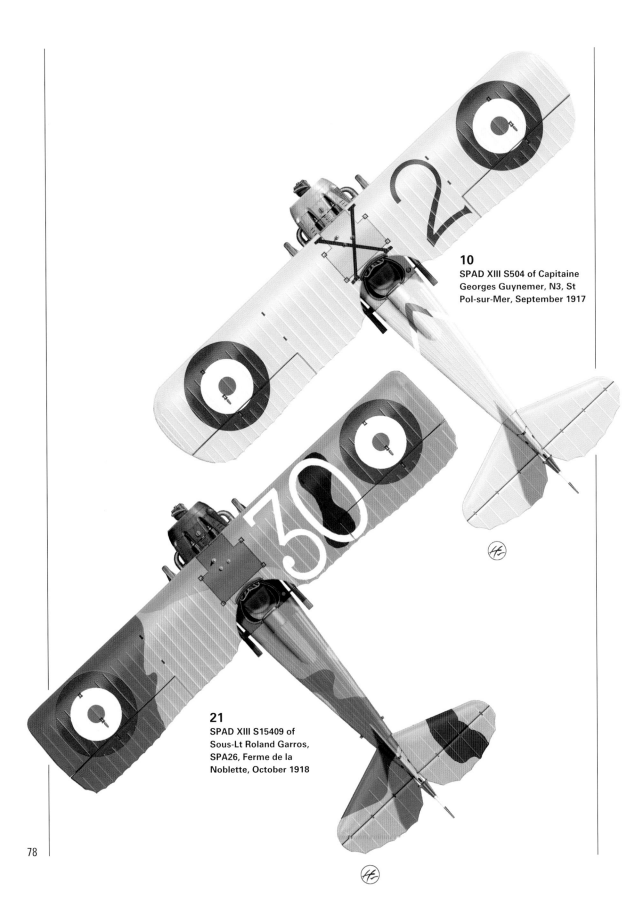

10
SPAD XIII S504 of Capitaine
Georges Guynemer, N3, St
Pol-sur-Mer, September 1917

21
SPAD XIII S15409 of
Sous-Lt Roland Garros,
SPA26, Ferme de la
Noblette, October 1918

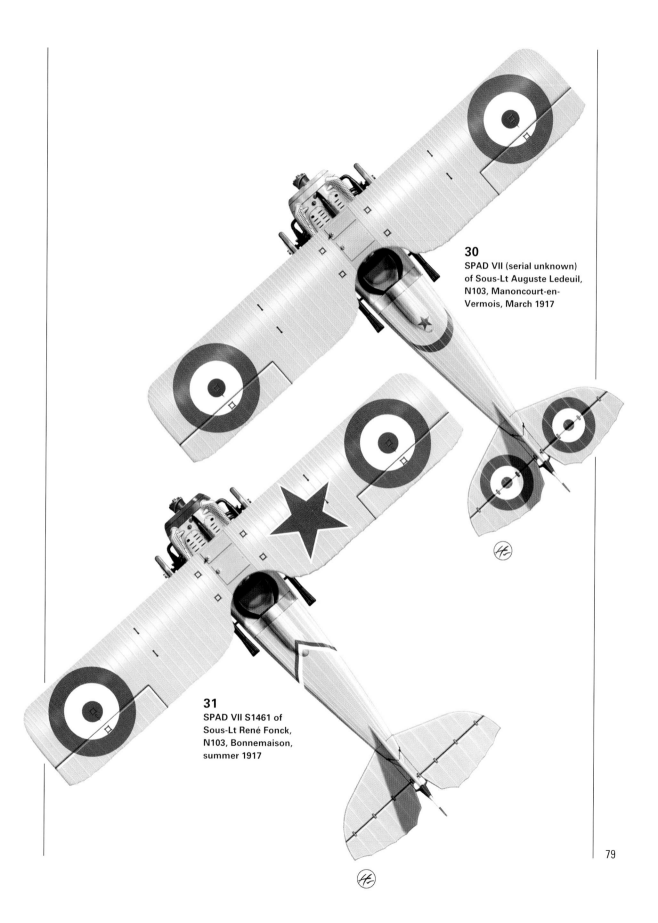

30
SPAD VII (serial unknown)
of Sous-Lt Auguste Ledeuil,
N103, Manoncourt-en-
Vermois, March 1917

31
SPAD VII S1461 of
Sous-Lt René Fonck,
N103, Bonnemaison,
summer 1917

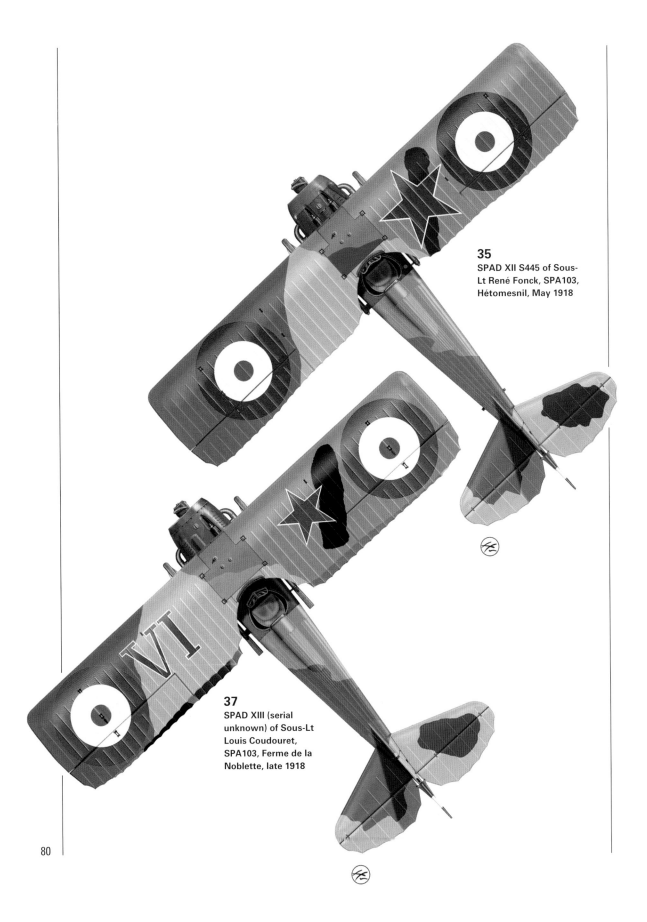

35
SPAD XII S445 of Sous-
Lt René Fonck, SPA103,
Hétomesnil, May 1918

37
SPAD XIII (serial
unknown) of Sous-Lt
Louis Coudouret,
SPA103, Ferme de la
Noblette, late 1918

SOLDIERING ON AFTER GUYNEMER

On 15 September 1917, GC11 began leaving Flanders for the VIer *Armée* sector, but GC12 continued to patrol, scoring two 'probables' and one confirmed victory – an enemy aeroplane downed in flames between Zonnebeke and Poelcapelle by Fonck. On the 18th, however, Sgt Reno was brought down by anti-aircraft fire. After his release from hospital and convalescent leave, he flew bombers with Br134 between 4 June and 18 July 1918, when he was commissioned an ensign in the US Naval Reserve Flying Corps.

On 19 September Brocard was assigned to serve as *Chef-de-Cabinet du Sous-secrétaire d'État à l'Aéronautique* in Paris. Capitaine d'Harcourt of N103 took temporary leadership of GC12 until command was formally passed on to Capitaine Henri Jacques Jean Horment, former commander of N62, on the 30th. Also on 19 September, Cpl Phelps Collins transferred to N103 from N313.

Born in Alpena, Michigan, in 1894, 'Eddie' Collins was the son of Richard H Collins, manufacturer of the Alpena Flyer automobile.

On 14 October 1917 Cpl Phelps Collins, a Lafayette Flying Corps (LFC) volunteer serving with SPA103, shot down an Albatros east of Langemarck. Promoted to sergent by the time he left the unit on 9 March 1918, he joined the 103rd Aero Squadron as a USAS captain, but was killed when his SPAD spun to the ground while searching for the German 'Paris gun' on 12 March *(Jon Guttman)*

Fonck downed a two-seater south of the Houthulst Forest on 23 September, possibly killing Uffz Rudolf Franke and Ltn Gustav Rudolf of Fl. Abt.(A) 6. GC12 moved back to Bierne on the 26th, and on the 27th Deullin scored his 18th victory. N26 suffered two casualties on the 28th, as MdL Noël Fontaine was wounded in both legs, while the SPAD (S1513) of MdL Jacques Mortureux caught fire at 200 metres altitude over the field and overturned upon landing, leaving him slightly burned.

GC12's worst month ended on a successful note, however, as Sgt Pierre Prou of N26 downed a two-seater over Poperinghe and Fonck teamed up with Adjutant Dupré of N102 to send another two-seater down in flames near La Lovie on the 30th. Fonck's description of the combat praised the coolness and skill of this adversary, and also claimed that when he visited the wreck he found papers identifying the dead pilot as 'Wissemann'.

Fonck subsequently told a visiting journalist that he had been 'the tool of retribution' for Guynemer's death. Fonck's lifelong claim to have personally avenged Guynemer has since been contradicted by the circumstances of Kurt Wissemann's actual death in a single-seat fighter two days earlier. Even Fonck's statement to the journalist about 'killing the murderer of my good friend' runs counter to the reality that while Guynemer may have known of, and even respected, Fonck in 1917, the two aces were never friends.

Hazy skies and high winds hindered the group in the first days of October, SPA3 losing Sgt René Gaillard when his SPAD collided with an RFC aeroplane and spun down to a fatal crash. With little opportunity for aerial combat, aircraft from N73 and N103 indulged in trench strafing on the 9th, and N26 and N103 strafed Merckem and German batteries in the Houthulst Forest on the 11th.

During a SPA3 patrol comprising Adjutant Ambroise Thomas and Brigadiers Xavier Andras de Marcy and André Dubonnet on the 14th, de Marcy spotted an Albatros two-seater and shot it down in flames near Bixschoote before his squadronmates could join in, killing Ltn Werner Hähne and Alfred Neuhaus of Fl. Abt. 40. Similarly, Cpl Collins peeled off from a six-aeroplane N103 patrol to dive on five Albatros D Vs out of the sun, sending one spinning down to crash near Poelkapelle, probably killing Offsv Rudolf Weckbrodt of *Jasta* 26. The remaining four Germans turned on Collins, but the timely arrival of British fighters persuaded them to disengage and retire to the east.

The 14th brought promotions at N73 – Deullin was made a capitaine and Adjutant-Chef François Bergot commissioned a sous-lieutenant – but the *escadrille* lost Sgt Gaston Drou, who was killed in SPAD VII S1760, possibly the tenth victory for Ltn Xaver Dannhuber of *Jasta* 26.

On 15 October Sgt Camille Piétri of N103 was credited with bringing down an enemy aeroplane over the Houthulst Forest, and another German was jointly filed as a 'probable' for a mixed patrol of GC12 fighters. N103 had another good day on 17 October, with Fonck downing two two-seaters over the Houthulst Forest and Sgts Lecomte and Turnure sharing in the destruction of another in the same location.

The next day saw Tenant de la Tour promoted to capitaine, but N73 suffered another casualty as MdL Pierre Jolivet was killed in SPAD S1118 by Ltn Walter von Bülow of *Jasta* 36. Fonck apparently had a run-in with the 'Circus' on the 21st, sending one of his opponents down in flames near

Sgt George Evans Turnure, another LFC member of SPA103, poses beside his SPAD VII. Turnure scored one victory with SPA103 on 17 October 1917, and added two more while serving in the 103rd Aero Squadron, USAS (*Jon Guttman*)

One of Capitaine Georges Raymond's SPAD VIIs, with the legend *'Ma Ninon'* barely visible below the cockpit. Taking command of SPA3 on 16 September 1917, Raymond did his bit to avenge Guynemer on 27 October, downing an enemy aeroplane over the Houthulst Forest for his fifth victory (*SHAA B91.515*)

Passchendaele, killing Vfw Fritz Bachmann of *Jasta* 6. To top the day off, Fonck was made a *Chevalier de la Légion d'Honneur*.

Sergent Robert Brière of SPA3 was wounded by flak on the 24th, but on 27 October the *escadrille* commander, Capitaine Raymond, scored his ace-making fifth victory and Fonck gained his 19th confirmed success. October ended with N73 and N103 being redesignated SPA73 and SPA103, respectively. The following week saw promotions and citations for a number of GC12 members. The most dramatic promotion went to Charles Biddle on 7 November, from sergent in the *Aviation Militaire* to captain in the US Army Air Service (USAS), although he would remain with SPA73 for some time to come.

Lt Paul Dumas was wounded on 5 November, but on the 8th Deullin claimed a Pfalz for his 19th victory. Detachments from SPA3, SPA26 and SPA103 began leaving the Dunkerque area for Maissonneuve, near Viller-Cotterets in the VIer *Armée* sector, on 11 November. SPA73 was still operating over Flanders the next day, however, when Lt Battesti sent an

Cpl Charles J Biddle is seen here with his SPAD VII of N73. Biddle was flying a new SPAD XIII when he scored his first victory on 5 December 1917. He subsequently transferred to the USAS, scoring his second victory in the 103rd Aero Squadron, raising his score to eight while leading the 13th Aero Squadron and finally commanding the Fourth Pursuit Group as a major (*Jack Eder Collection via Jon Guttman*)

enemy aeroplane crashing west of the Houthulst Forest for his third victory, killing Uffz Emil Herrlich and Ltn Kurt Flintzer of Fl. Abt.(A) 277. However, Capitaine Duval, who had joined SPA73 just two weeks earlier, was killed on the same day in a take-off accident in SPAD VII S1641.

On 17 November Cpl Frank Leaman Baylies reported to SPA73. Born in New Bedford, Massachusetts, on 23 September 1895, Baylies had volunteered for the ambulance service in May 1916, serving at the Somme, Verdun and in Serbia before joining the LFC. As the 13th pilot on SPA73's roster at the time, he was assigned SPAD XIII '13'. 'Cannot afford to be superstitious – nothing like being a fatalist,' he wrote in a letter home.

SPAD VII S1832 landed in error at Bergen op Zoom in the neutral Netherlands on 18 November 1917. Its pilot, MdL Louis Paoli of N73, was interned (*Jon Guttman*)

A cousin of N73's Corsican ace François Battesti, Louis Paoli escaped from the Netherlands on 9 January 1918 and rejoined SPA73 – now no longer part of GC12 – on 7 March. He was killed in action over Quennevières on 22 August 1918 by Ltn d R Werner Peckmann of *Jasta* 9 (*Jon Guttman*)

Baylies was not remiss in such a philosophy, for on the very next day one of his squadron mates, MdL Louis Paoli, became disoriented and landed in the neutral Netherlands, where he and his SPAD VII (S1832) were interned. Paoli, who was François Battesti's cousin, later escaped and rejoined SPA73, but was killed in action on 22 August 1918. November ended on a sour note with Sgt Jean Dedieu of SPA26 being injured in an accident on the 29th, but on 1 December SPA73 got an American replacement for Paoli in the person of Cpl Edward David Judd, a 23-year-old LFC volunteer from Boston, Massachusetts.

On 5 December Capt Biddle, using a new SPAD XIII, finally opened his account by shooting down an Albatros two-seater, which he reported last seeing on its back near Langemarck. The crew, Ltn Fritz Pauly and Ernst Sauter of Fl. Abt. 45, were killed. Lt Paul Tourtel of SPA103 was flying a SPAD XIII on the 8th when he became lost in fog and suffered a fatal crash near Crépy-en-Valois. By the 12th, with the Third Battle of Ypres finally over, the remaining elements of GC12 had moved to Maissonneuve.

Yet another of GC12's earliest heroes lost his life on 17 December when Capitaine Mathieu Tenant de la Tour, victor over nine enemy aeroplanes,

First joining SPA73 on 1 December 1917, Cpl David E Judd transferred to SPA3 on the 18th and remained there until 22 July, when he joined the US Navy. He also flew bombers with No 218 Sqn, Royal Air Force (*Jon Guttman*)

was killed in an accident while flying a new SPAD XIII at Auchel. Lt Daniel Dumêmes took acting command of SPA26 until de la Tour's official successor, Lt Xavier de Sevin, transferred over from N12 on Christmas Day.

One day after losing its commander, SPA26 got a pleasant surprise when MdL Benjamin de Tascher reported for duty – again. Taken prisoner on 12 April, he had managed to escape from the PoW camp at Dillingen on 10 September, made his way to Switzerland and eventually returned to France. Henceforth, he would be nicknamed 'The Fugitive' by his squadronmates.

Also on 18 December, SPA3 got its first Americans when Cpls David Judd and Frank Baylies transferred from SPA73. After a month of patrolling as opportunity permitted, and amassing experience, 'Jules' Baylies, as his squadronmates came to call him, was destined to be SPA3's top-scoring ace of 1918.

On 17 December another noted GC12 ace was lost when SPA26's commander, Capitaine Mathieu Tenant de la Tour, was killed in a flying accident (Greg VanWyndgarden)

NEW YEAR, NEW ORGANISATION

GC12's last confirmed victory in 1917 was scored by Adjutant Naudin of SPA26 on 29 December. With the New Year came a new air base, as the Storks were ordered to Beauzée-sur-Aire, the move being made between 10 and 16 January 1918. There was also a change in group make-up, as SPA67 arrived at Beauzée on the 16th to replace SPA.73, which was in turn detached from GC12 and combined with SPA85, SPA95 and SPA96 to form GC19.

Capitaine Deullin took command of GC19 on 7 February 1918, while Capitaine Pierre Cahuzac took over leadership of SPA73. The newly created GC19 was in turn amalgamated within a new expansion of the group principle, *Escadre de Combat No 1*, which also comprised GC15 (SPA37, SPA81, SPA93 and SPA97) and GC18 (SPA48, SPA94, SPA153 and SPA155). Commanded by *Chef de Bataillon* Victor Ménard, former commander of N26 and GC15, the new *escadre* could field 12 squadrons wherever they might be needed to achieve local air superiority.

Lt Alfred Rougevin-Baville of SPA67 climbs aboard his SPAD VII, which displays the unit's original eagle on a pennant motif. On 19 January 1918, SPA67 joined GC12 to replace SPA73, which formed the nucleus of the new GC19 along with SPA85, SPA95 and SPA96. Soon afterward, the unit's emblem was revised to conform to the common group theme (*SHAA B87.2056*)

87

Several members of SPA73 went on to greater things after the unit left GC12. Actively leading GC19, Deullin shot down an Albatros east of Montdidier on 19 May 1918 for his 20th, and last, victory. He survived the war, but was killed on 29 May 1923 while testing a prototype aeroplane at Villacoublay.

Charles Biddle left SPA73 to join SPA124 *Lafayette Escadrille* on 10 January, followed on the 21st by Maury Jones. By the time the two Americans arrived, SPA124's American personnel had been reassigned en masse to the USAS, and their unit redesignated the 103rd Aero Squadron. Biddle would score another victory with the 103rd, then command the 13th Aero Squadron, with whom he downed six more enemy aeroplanes, and finally be put in command of the 4th Pursuit Group, with the rank of major.

Although Maury Jones was not credited with any aerial victories, his experience and leadership abilities led to his being given command of the 28th Aero Squadron. SPA73's Corsican ace, François Battesti, brought his total up to seven while flying the SPAD XIII, XII and XVII. Made a *Chevalier de la Légion d'Honneur*, he published a small memoir, *Les Cigognes de Brocard en combat*, two years before dying in his hometown of Azzana on 24 August 1977.

Escadrille 67 had originally been founded on 17 September 1915, with Sous-Lt Tenant de la Tour as its first commander until 21 September. The unit had gained fame during the Battle of Verdun through the efforts of Sous-Lt Jean Navarre, who scored seven of his 12 victories while in N67, MdL Georges Flachaire, who was credited with eight, and Sous-Lt Marcel

On 21 January 1918, C Maury Jones departed SPA73 to join N124 *Lafayette*. By the time he arrived, its American personnel had been transferred to the USAS and the unit redesignated the 103rd Aero Squadron (*Jack Eder Collection*)

Viallet, with six. By January 1918, SPA67, under the command of Capitaine Marie Jacques d'Indy, had 28 confirmed victories in its squadron log, for the loss of five pilots missing, seven wounded and one injured in an accident. With its incorporation in GC12, SPA67's insignia – an eagle within an orange and red pennant – was altered to a larger, red and black pennant bearing a stork in the flight attitude of SPA3's.

Amid the reorganisation, combat operations continued. The first confirmed victories for GC12 in 1918 were scored by Fonck, when he

Like his old *escadrille* mate Charlie Biddle, Maury Jones went on to bigger things in the USAS as commander of the 28th Aero Squadron. Captain Jones is shown here beside his SPAD, S7833 (*Jon Guttman*)

Credited with 28 victories before being attached to GC12, SPA67 was commanded by Capitaine Marie Jacques d'Indy (left), shown with Lt Cherel during earlier service in C30 (*B92.1751*)

downed two fighters on 19 January. The next day, Lt de Sevin and MdL Noël Fontaine came to the aid of a Breguet 14A2 of Br35, and both SPA26 pilots, as well as the Breguet crew, were credited with the destruction of one of its attackers near Samoneux. It was de Sevin's first success since taking command of the *escadrille*, and his seventh overall.

On the same day, however, Cpl Henry Augustus Batchelor III – an LFC pilot from Saginaw, Michigan, who had joined SPA103 on 26 December – was injured in an accident. By the time he recovered, he had transferred to US Naval Aviation as an ensign on 3 March. Fellow LFC member David Judd left SPA3 on 22 January after being commissioned an ensign in the US Navy. He subsequently flew anti-submarine patrols in float-planes from Dunkerque and bombing missions with No 218 Sqn, RAF, before serving on the staff of the US Navy's Northern Bombing Group.

SPA67 opened its account with GC12 on 25 January when Adjutant Marcel Duret brought down an Albatros D V near Béthincourt at 1515 hrs. Also participating in the engagement was Cpl Philip Phillips Benney, a 22-year-old LFC volunteer from Pittsburgh, Pennsylvania, who had been with SPA67 since 12 December, and of whom d'Indy had commented, 'So ardent was he that I had long delayed the moment of sending him against the enemy, fearing a little too much audacity and too little experience.'

Benney was credited with damaging an Albatros, but he was grievously wounded in the calf and thigh over Montfaucon, probably by Ltn d R Otto Kissenberth of *Jasta* 23b. After force landing 500 metres west of Fort Choisel, Benney was rushed to the hospital at Glorieux, but succumbed to his wounds the following day. He was posthumously awarded the *Croix de Guerre* with palm.

A break in winter weather brought mixed fortunes on 5 February. During a patrol between Clermont-en-Argonne and Varennes-en-

This Blériot-built SPAD XIII of an unidentified pilot displays the later unit insignia of SPA67, which took the form of SPA3's stork within a black and red pennant (*SHAA B85.2137*)

Argonne, Fonck sent a two-seater down in pieces and Haegelen forced another to dive for German lines with its observer either dead or wounded, but Cpl William Hallett Tailer, an LFC volunteer from Roslyn, New York, who had joined SPA67 on 14 December, was hit and killed by anti-aircraft fire over Montzéville. On the 7th, Adjutant Marcel Haegelen left SPA103 for SPA100, with which unit he would raise his score from two to 22, including 15 balloons, and Lt Jean Thobie departed SPA67 to command SPA48, subsequently being reassigned to command SPA156 on 23 July 1918.

On 16 February Sous-Lts Bozon-Verduraz and Guy Gonzague de la Rochfordière downed an aeroplane east of Damloup – the first victory for both pilots – and Bozon-Verduraz claimed a two-seater the next day. 'Bozon-Verduraz was a very bad pilot,' his friend Risacher stated, 'but he had fantastic courage. When he was attacking a German, he would be shouting, *"Pas encore, pas encore!"* He did not manoeuvre at all! He came right up to the Huns, shot for a few minutes, would not do a half-turn, just went straight on, coming back with his gloves and flying suit shot full of holes. He knew he was a bad shot and a very bad pilot, so he would wait until the last moment, say ten or fifteen metres, before he would shoot.

'Lt de la Rochefordière was a very fine fellow, but he disappeared very quickly,' Risacher added. 'He wasn't a fighter. He was very courageous, but he was not a fighter. When he brought down a German, Bozon-Verduraz kept credit for himself, but he agreed to share credit for two with de la Rochefordière.'

The 17th saw another American leave SPA67, but in this case Cpl William T Ponder, an LFC volunteer from Llano, Texas, was merely transferring to SPA163, where he was promoted to first lieutenant in the USAS ten days later. 'Wild Bill' Ponder would go on to score three victories with SPA163 and another three with the 103rd Aero Squadron,

Recovered from injuries sustained in a crash on 24 July 1917, MdL Edouard Moulines sits proudly atop his new SPAD XIII after rejoining SPA3. Note that the number '14' is repeated on the left of the upper wing, rather than the usual right (*Louis Risacher album via Jon Guttman*)

as well as being awarded the *Croix de Guerre* with four palms and the Distinguished Service Cross.

Fonck downed an Albatros D V on 18 February and a two-seater on the 19th, while Cpl Baylies of SPA3 opened his account with a two-seater in flames north of Forges. 'It was mighty exciting', he remarked in a letter home, 'much better than duck shooting and much more profitable.' Bozon-Verduraz and de la Rochfordière sent a two-seater down in flames near Les Eparges on the 20th, while Capitaine Raymond eliminated another two-seater north of Vauquois for his sixth confirmed victory. Fonck accounted for two two-seaters within 15 minutes on the 26th.

On that same day, SPA3 got another American in the person of Adjutant Edwin Charles Parsons. Born in Holyoke, Massachusetts, on 24 September 1892, 'Ted' Parsons had learned to fly in 1912, and had briefly taken up an offer from Mexican revolutionary Francisco 'Pancho' Villa to train airmen, but made a hasty exit after he learned of Villa's raid on Columbus, New Mexico. Later serving in the famed N124 *Lafayette*, he downed a Rumpler on 4 September 1917, and chose to remain with the French when his unit was transferred to the USAS on 18 February 1918.

Commenting on SPA3's Americans, Louis Risacher opined:

'I had none but the greatest admiration for Baylies. Edwin Parsons I didn't appreciate much. David Judd I thought was a nice boy, but he didn't stay with the squadron long.'

Amid another period of bad weather, the only Serbian airman to fight over the Western Front reported to SPA3 on 1 March. Born to a wealthy family in Belgrade on 19 February 1892, Lt Tadija R Sondrmajer had cut short his technical studies in Germany to take part in the Balkan Wars of 1912–13, then served in the cavalry in 1914. In 1916 he flew as an observer in Maurice Farmans with Serbian *escadrille* MF521 over Macedonia, before qualifying as a pilot in June 1917. Contracting malaria in

Lt Pierre Pendaries sits in his SPAD VII *"MOUSTIC V"* while with N69, the future ace using this machine to score his first three victories. Joining SPA67 in February 1918, he had increased his tally to seven by the end of the war (*Steve St Martin Collection via Jon Guttman*)

November, he was sent to hospital in France for three months' convalescence, during which time he undertook fighter training at Pau and Cazeaux, and met René Fonck, who persuaded him to join the Storks.

Xavier de Sevin was promoted to *capitaine* on 2 March, and GC12 subsequently moved from Beauzée-sur-Aire to Lhéry, about 20 kilometres west-southwest of Reims, to support Général Marie Eugène Debeney's I*er Armée*. Baylies scored his second victory northeast of Courtecon on the 7th, but the following week saw some group members venturing down to strafe enemy troops, along with three crashes, fortunately without injury.

Aerial combat resumed on 15 March, with Fonck downing two two-seaters, and fellow SPA103 pilot Sgt Pierre Schmitter dispatching another for his first victory. The next day saw a two-seater downed in flames by Fonck, a fighter sent spiralling down over Chevrigny by the recently promoted Sgt Baylies and an Albatros D V in flames by Sgt Auguste Baux of SPA103. Sous-Lt Emile Letourneau of SPA26 forced a German two-seater to land, but had to do the same after its observer put a disabling round in his engine. A Pfalz D III on the 17th brought Fonck's score up to 30, while a two-seater became the second victory for Adjutant Adrien Mion of SPA67 on the same date.

Sgt Pierre Schmitter of SPA103 leans against his Blériot-built SPAD XIII. After downing an enemy two-seater on 15 March 1918, he established a reputation for reliability in the squadron, finishing the war with three confirmed victories (*SHAA B67.500*)

KAISERSCHLACHT

GC12's on-and-off activity since its hard times in Flanders seemed to be a form of retraining for new challenges when a fresh crisis arose on 21 March 1918. On that day the Germans, with the Italian army thrown back to the Piave River and revolution-racked Russia out of the war, launched Operation *Michael*, which was the first of a succession of offensives later collectively called *der Kaiserschlacht* ('Kaiser's Battle'). Its ultimate objectives were to rout the Portuguese Army, cut off and destroy the British Expeditionary Force and drive on to take Paris before the American Expeditionary Force could arrive on the Western Front in full strength.

Louis Risacher recalled that on 21 March, 'I was in Paris with two very dear friends of mine, Frank Baylies and an English infantry major, C D Lacey. He was a solicitor in Dorset. I had known him for years from school. He had joined the British Army as a volunteer, and was, just now, in Paris. We were having lunch at my place with my father and mother, and having a very good meal, which was rare in those days, when we heard the newsboys shouting. My father called the maid and told her to fetch a paper. So she came back with a paper, with the title printed in big letters, *GERMANS ATTACK ON THE SOMME FRONT*. They had already advanced several kilometres. Bad news. Lacey had just been telling us that

Lt Louis Risacher and Sgt André Dubonnet stand before a SPAD XIII of SPA3 (*SHAA B82.735*)

if the Germans attacked that spot he would have been killed in the trenches. He looked at me, Baylies looked at me – we understood one another at once. We stopped our lunch and, after kissing my people, we went out to rejoin our units, Lacey to his unit, Baylies and I to the Stork Squadron.'

The main German threat to the French was around the town of Montdidier. GC12's activities on the offensive's first overcast day included Adjutants Baux, Joseph Baron and Gaston Tasqué of SPA103 forcing a Rumpler down with a punctured fuel tank near Rilly-le-Montagne, where its wounded crew was taken prisoner.

In the days thereafter, however, the group had to withdraw, along with the I*ére Armée*. While fighting continued in the air on the 22nd, SPA26 moved to Mesnil-St Georges. On the 23rd Tasqué was killed in an accident, while the Germans advanced far enough for a giant specialised artillery piece they had developed to lob shells into the suburbs of Paris, 75 miles away. SPA3 and SPA103 fell back on Mesnil-St Georges on the 24th, followed by SPA67 on the 25th. The next day saw SPA3, SPA26 and SPA67 moved to Raray.

Amid the retreat, Ted Parsons recounted a tale of how Frank Baylies' fighting career almost suffered an embarrassing premature termination. He had been carousing too late the night before, and when the time came for the dawn patrol, he was barely able to leap out of bed, throw cold water on his face, pull his *combinaison* over his pyjamas and rush over to his aeroplane in time to join his flight, led by a cursing Lt Raymond.

Zealous to redeem himself at some German's expense, Baylies stayed up longer than the rest, until he noticed that his SPAD XIII was almost out of fuel and he headed back to the aerodrome, his mind now fixed on breakfast and gallons of hot coffee. As his aeroplane landed, however, Baylies noticed an unusual amount of chaotic activity on the field, as well as a lot of aeroplanes of unfamiliar configuration. As he taxied toward his hangar, he spotted the black crosses on the new aeroplanes and realised the chilling truth. The Germans had just overrun the aerodrome. His quarters, his new dress uniform with 150 francs in the pocket of his tunic and his newly bought English boots and Sam Browne belt were just metres away, but they may as well have been kilometres for all likelihood Baylies had of retrieving those items.

Baylies took what he saw as his only option – he gunned the motor, spun his aeroplane around in a half ground loop and headed full throttle back down the runway, while two of the swifter-moving Germans caught hold of his wings and shouted for him to surrender. At that point, Baylies almost had to comply, as the roar of his motor faded to a dying sputter. Watching his pressure gauge sink toward zero, Baylies cursed himself for forgetting his auxiliary tank, switched to gravity feed and was relieved to see the pressure needle swing back up to 150. As the SPAD picked up speed the Germans hung on as best they could, loping along the field until first one and then the other let go and somersaulted along the ground to a bruising stop in Baylies' wake.

Finally getting airborne amid a fusillade of rifle fire, Baylies ascended to 300 metres' altitude and glided in for a landing at GC12's new airfield ten minutes later. There, his squadronmates confirmed that the Germans had indeed just overrun the old aerodrome, and that the *méchanos* had driven

Sous-Lt Fonck returns from a successful sortie in which he brought down a Rumpler C IV in French lines (*SHAA B76.27*)

off with all the equipment they could quickly salvage in their trucks, while the pilots took off with nothing more than what they could carry in their cockpits.

Sous-Lt André Willemin of SPA67 failed to return from a patrol on 27 March, and at about that same time Capitaine d'Harcourt left SPA103 to take command of GC13. His 24-year-old successor, Ltn Joseph Battle, had been a soldier since 1912. He enrolled in the air service on 15 November 1916, and had served in N77 since 6 April 1917, scoring one victory before his transfer to SPA103.

Battle got a swift demonstration of his unit's capabilities on 28 March, as Fonck sent a two-seater down in flames east of Montdidier, but the new commander was wounded in the foot by ground fire that morning. Another victim of ground fire that day was Baylies, who described his experience as 'a real dime novel affair'.

He had fired three rounds at an enemy two-seater over Montdidier when his engine stopped, its magneto wire severed by a bullet. Under fire from the enemy observer, 'and every German soldier who could aim a rifle', Baylies glided to a rough landing in no man's land, 60 yards from a large detachment of German soldiers, and 100 yards from the French lines. Baylies proceeded to make what he called the fastest sprint of his life while French troops shot one of the three Germans who pursued him. He made it to safety, and the enemy soldiers contented themselves with destroying his SPAD. Baylies was probably credited to Vfw Gehrke and Ltn von Jena of Fl. Abt. 44, but he was cited for his escape, especially since he had taken the time to recover the altimeter and watch from his aeroplane before abandoning it!

The 29th saw Fonck dispatch two German fighters in five minutes east of Montdidier. On that same day, Cpl Jasper Cornish Brown – a New Yorker who had joined SPA67 through the LFC on 3 February – was promoted to second lieutenant in the USAS, but remained with the *escadrille* throughout the war.

April began with victories for Sgt Gilbert Loup of SPA103 and for Capitaine de Sevin and Cpl Désiré Mabereau of SPA26, the latter of whom was promoted to sergent the next day. Three 'probables' were scored by SPA3 and SPA26 on 3 April, but the latter unit lost Sgt Pierre Devaulx over Montdidier to Ltn Fritz Pütter of *Jasta* 68, and Cpl Pierre Bernard of SPA67 was wounded in action. Rain cancelled operations for a few days, but during that respite Benjamin Bozon-Verduraz was made a *Chevalier de la Légion d'Honneur*.

On 8 April SPA67 and SPA103 moved to Hétomesnil in the sector of Général Georges Louis Humbert's III*er Armée*, followed by SPA3 and SPA26 the next day. Baylies sent an artillery spotting aeroplane down in flames on 11 April and became an ace the next day by sending another two-seater crashing to earth. Fonck also scored on 12 April, driving down a scout on fire at 1330 hrs, followed by a two-seater 15 minutes later.

Poor weather and even snow flurries curtailed GC12's scoring until 20 April, when Sous-Lt Alfred Rougevin-Baville and Adjutant Edmond Jacques Marcel Pillon of SPA67 brought down an enemy aeroplane and Bozon-Verduraz downed another. The 25-year-old Pillon had only joined SPA67 five days earlier, but he was already an ace, having scored his first victory on 2 August 1916 while with N102, and four more in 1917 with N82.

At 0815 hrs on 21 April, a SPA67 patrol attacked a German aeroplane between Thory and Rouvel, joined by Bozon-Verduraz, whose gunfire set it afire. Bozon-Verduraz's ace-making fifth kill was shared with SPA67

The Rumpler C IV brought down by Fonck shows a wing cross in the process of being converted from Maltese style to the straight-sided *Balkenkreuz* during the opening phase of the last German offensive in late March 1918 (*SHAA B76.32*)

Adjutant Edmond Pillon of SPA67 (right) with Adjutant Marchal. Joining SPA67 on 15 April, Pillon scored two of his eight victories with that squadron (*Greg VanWyngarden*)

members Sous-Lt Duret, Adjutant Mion and Brigadier Max Ouvrard de Linière. Sous-Lt Bucquet of SPA3 also downed a two-seater near Roye that day, but such events were overshadowed by another German loss elsewhere – Rittmeister Manfred *Freiherr* von Richthofen, commander of JG I and victor over 80 Allied aircraft, had been killed in action over Morlancourt Ridge.

Fonck scored his 36th victory on 22 April, and on the 24th Parsons returned from leave in the United States. 'From the first,' Parsons wrote in retrospect, 'I could feel the atmosphere of camaraderie and pride in SPA3. The *"Vieux Charles"*, Guynemer the incomparable, was gone, but in some indefinable way his spirit seemed to hover over and guide the entire personnel from officers to mechanics.'

April ended with the now-aggressive Lt de la Rochfordière being reassigned to take command of SPA94.

The first success for May occurred on the 2nd when Baylies, returning from a patrol in Bozon-Verduraz's SPAD XIII, spotted three Rumplers overhead. He stood the SPAD on its tail and, in his own words, 'let Mr

André Dubonnet trains in a Blériot XI. Being the scion of the wine-making family made him a guaranteed asset when he joined SPA3 on 29 April 1918, but Dubonnet went on to be a six-victory ace as well (*Jon Guttman*)

Hun have the benefit of two perfectly-working, well-regulated machine guns. He didn't have much to say and fell out of control, hit the ground with an awful blow and lay there a crumpled mass of debris.'

Jammed guns the next morning resulted in Baylies having to settle for seeing his quarry forced to land in German lines, but that afternoon he and MdL André Dubonnet, 20-year-old scion of the Parisian wine-producing family, shot a two-seater down in flames just outside of Montdidier, killing Ltns Willi Karbe and Erich Meuche of Fl. Abt.(A) 245. Sgt Mabereau was killed that day, however, probably by Ltn Carl Galetschky of *Jasta* 48, and on the 4th Cpl Marcel Dupont was wounded in the foot, possibly by Ltn Karl Odebrett of *Jasta* 42. GC12 underwent a change of leadership on 4 May, with Capitaine Horment passing command to Capitaine Charles Dupuy, a veteran of N48, N351 and N31, and a *Chevalier de la Légion d'Honneur*.

Ted Parsons opened his account with SPA3 by downing a two-seater on 6 May. The 9th saw Raymond promoted to Capitaine and GC12's pilots flying 65 sorties, but the highlight of the day occurred after Baylies and Parsons, annoyed by Fonck's high-handed lecturing on tactics, made a wager that would have unexpectedly notable consequences. Parsons later wrote that it had come about while he and Baylies were at the *Club des Cigognes* (more often referred to simply as 'Le Bar') with Walter Duranty of the *New York Sun* and Paul Rockwell of the *Chicago Daily News*.

'Then René Fonck of 103 came in and was asked to join us,' Parsons recounted, 'which of course he did promptly, never having been known to say "No". The only thing that ever worried Fonck was that he wouldn't hear someone ask him. Somehow, undoubtedly egged on by Rockwell, we began a discussion as to our relative merits. Being full of ambition and good cheer, Baylies and I bet Fonck a bottle of champagne that on the patrol on which we were all leaving shortly, we would get a Hun before he did.'

'When Frank and I got to the lines,' Parsons wrote, 'we found a whole mess of greasy weather had blown up, and there was a rotten yellow haze that made visibility most difficult.' The two lost contact, but Parsons – remarking in retrospect, 'I was willing to take almost any kind of a chance to stick Fonck for a bottle of champagne' – carried on alone, making an unsuccessful attempt to pursue a German formation flying at more than 18,000 ft over enemy territory.

Returning to a more comfortable 12,000 ft, he spotted a Halberstadt CL II and was about to dive on it when he saw another SPAD attack it from the side, and recognised the stork and number on the fuselage side – Baylies. Parsons claimed to have joined Baylies in catching the Halberstadt 'in a merciless crossfire' until it went down shedding its wings between Gratibus and Braches, but only Baylies was credited with its destruction, for his eighth confirmed victory. Reporting their success to the reporters less than an hour after taking off, Parsons said:

'They played up to us in great shape, and we were cocks of the walk till we heard the familiar staccato motor signal above the field, which meant that someone who had brought down a Boche was coming in. It was Fonck, and although we had beaten him on time and gotten our Boche first, he took every bit of the wind out of our sails in short order.'

Like Parsons, Fonck complained of the thick ground fog that morning. 'At about 1500 hrs the fog began to disperse,' he wrote in *Mes Combats*, 'and three quarters of an hour later I was able to take off in the company of Capitaine Battle and Sous-Lt Fontaine. Scarcely out of our lines, we fell upon an enemy patrol composed of a reconnaissance aeroplane protected by a pair of two-seater fighter aeroplanes. In a manoeuvre planned in advance, I immediately gave the signal to attack, and facing an enemy pilot, I shot him down with the first burst of fire.

'I gave no further thought to him in order to remain alert, and avoid being shot down by his comrades. I went into a rapid turn, followed by a dive. Thus I placed myself under the wing of another Boche, whose machine gun was trying to get at me, but he was too late. A second time I opened fire and my next opponent tumbled down, while the third was doing his best to escape from my comrades.'

The third two-seater dived, but Fonck was on its tail in seconds, sending it down in pieces over Grivesne, south of Moreuil, at 1600 hrs. Fonck claimed that the entire combat had taken 45 seconds, and that the Germans fell within 400 metres of each other. The official account stated that the first two had fallen within ten seconds of each other and the third crashed five minutes later, at 1605 hrs. Either way, Parsons could see that, 'he had made a real record for the boys to write about, besides which our little stunt paled into insignificance'.

But the afternoon was not over yet. In a second patrol with Sous-Lt Léon Thouzellier and Sgt Jean Brugère, Fonck attacked another two-seater at 1820 hrs and saw it break up over Montdidier. Although he lost sight of his two comrades, Fonck later wrote that he preferred hunting alone. 'I never try to let a comrade down, but above all, I like my freedom of action, for it is indispensable for the success of my undertakings.' He then attacked four Fokkers and five Albatros two-seaters at 1855 hrs, and dispatched two of the escorts in flames in a matter of eight seconds, killing Ltn Ernst Schulze and Uffz Otto Kutter of *Jasta* 48.

Fonck had won the champagne with a phenomenal six victories in one afternoon. In curious contrast to Parsons, however, he never mentioned the wager in his memoirs, writing only that, 'I had been dreaming for some time of shooting down five adversaries within a 24-hour period'.

Among the wingmen who frequently flew patrols with Fonck in SPA103 was Sous-Lt Léon Thouzellier, who had previously flown Maurice Farman reconnaissance aeroplanes with MF58 (*SHAA B86.4376*)

MdL Edouard Moulines with his SPAD XIII. On 16 May 1918, he scored his second victory, shared with Lt Bozon-Verduraz and Sgt Risacher (*Louis Risacher album via Jon Guttman*)

Baylies and MdL Georges Clément downed a two-seater on 10 May, while Dubonnet got another. Clear skies on 15 May brought five victories to GC12, starting with a scout in flames at 0825 hrs, shared between Brigadier Max Ouvrard de Linière of SPA67 and Capitaine Jacques Sabattier de Vignolle, the commander of GC18. Bozon-Verduraz and MdL Edouard Moulines of SPA3 downed a two-seater near Assainvillers at 1135 hrs, and at 1225 hrs SPA26 accounted for two – one by de Sevin, Sous-Lt de Tascher and Adjutant Julius Antoine, and the other by Lts Letourneau and Jean Marie Auguste Dombray. Sgt Piétri of SPA103 finished a fruitful day at 1955 hrs by scoring his second victory near Moreuil.

Another good flying day began on a sour note when Sous-Lt Charles Albanel of SPA3 failed to return from an 0800 hrs patrol on 16 May, the *escadrille's* first loss of the year. Albanel eventually turned up as a PoW, having been credited as the first of an eventual 25 victories for Ltn Max Näther of *Jasta* 62. SPA3 got its revenge later that day as Parsons, MdL Jean Denneulin and Sgt Maurice Chevannes downed a two-seater, and Risacher scored his first confirmed success – an enemy fighter – in concert with Bozon-Verduraz and Moulines. SPA26 also added a shared victory to its tally, for de Sevin's tenth and Lt Jacques Puget's first.

Their 16 May kill was the first of three that would be shared between Parsons and the handsome Denneulin, with whom Parsons said he developed a 'hunter-killer technique'. This involved Denneulin flying

50 metres above and to the right or left of Parsons. 'I never had to look. He was always there,' Parsons said. 'If he spotted enemy aeroplanes which might endanger us, he'd sweep down waggling his wings and pointing to the danger zone. If I spotted our quarry, I'd waggle and we'd go into the attack.' It is interesting to note that the teamwork between Parsons and Denneulin bears a remarkable resemblance to the basic *Rotte* credited to future German ace Werner Mölders during the Spanish Civil War, almost 20 years later.

Sous-Lt Pierre Pendaries of SPA67, who had scored three previous victories while serving in N69, downed a two-seater northeast of Moreuil on 17 May, while Sgts Loup and Henri Drouillh of SPA103 bagged a Pfalz D IIIa near Montdidier. Adjutant Pillon of SPA67 sent a two-seater crashing east of Montdidier on the 18th.

A few cannon-armed SPAD XIIs had made their way to GC12 since the type's spotty debut in Guynemer's hands, including one for SPA3 – probably flown by Raymond or Benjamin Bozon-Verduraz – and two (S445 and S452) to SPA103, where they were almost exclusively flown by Fonck. If ever man and machine were made for each other, Fonck and the cannon SPAD were. Yet his first combat in the new scout, while leading Lt Thouzellier and Sgt Brugère on patrol on 19 May, almost proved to be his last.

'At about 4500 metres up, we came upon a Boche patrol composed of five aeroplanes, two of which were two-seater fighters,' Fonck wrote.

'Despite numbers, we did not hesitate to offer battle. I succeeded in manoeuvring above them, then quickly plunged into the group in a vertical dive. Before he knew what was happening to him, for I was hardly 50 metres behind him, I sent a volley of 20 bullets into the rear of the fifth pilot. That was enough for me to have the satisfaction of seeing him nose

Sous-Lt Fonck climbs aboard S445, which was one of two SPAD XIIs armed with 37 mm cannon to be assigned to SPA103 and flown primarily by him, in May 1918 (*SHAA B76.23*)

Fonck stands beside SPAD XII S452, which was the second cannon SPAD assigned to SPA103 (*Louis Risacher album via Jon Guttman*)

down and go into the spiral. Then, immediately straightening out, I raced on to the next closest aeroplane. It did not take long. With a burst of machine-gun fire I put an end to his career.

'For his part, my buddy Brugère brought down another one, but Thouzellier, having engine trouble, was at grips with the last two, who furiously tailed him and riddled him with bullets in his descent. Seeing him in such a bad spot, I tried to relieve him by a rapid turn, but as I was flying upside down, my extra cartridges, placed at my side in a case, fell among the controls and one of them got wedged in.

'I felt myself tearing through the air on my back at full speed,' Fonck continued, 'and I was afraid at any instant that I would be shot down by the German whom I was about to attack, and who, realising my critical

Sous-Lt Louis Fernand Coudouret stands beside his SPAD XIII, which had been somewhat pranged on landing in April 1918. Already credited with five enemy aeroplanes from previous units – including three over Russia with N581 – Coudouret scored his sixth victory in concert with Sgt Robert B Hoeber, an LFC member of SPA103, on 2 June 1918 (*SHAA B85.2119*)

situation, would follow me firing away with his machine gun. I was carrying a new SPAD test gun for the first time, and I also did not know how to manoeuvre in order to get out of this predicament. Believing my situation to be hopeless, I resolved to risk everything. I abandoned the controls and picked up the scattered shells, which I threw over the side one by one. The few seconds this operation took seemed like an eternity to me, but I was finally able to straighten out 1000 metres below. Never before did I feel death pass by so closely.'

One of the two enemy two-seaters claimed by Fonck in that fight – using the SPAD XII's machine gun without resorting to the cannon, it might be noted – probably resulted in the deaths of Uffz Walter Graaf and Sgt Christian Höfele near Montdidier, while Brugère was credited with one of the fighter escorts. Fonck eventually claimed 11 of his victories in the cannon SPAD, of which seven were confirmed.

In addition to those successes Sous-Lt Louis Fernand Coudouret, who had just joined SPA103 the day before, helped two SPA153 pilots force a German scout down, while the SPA3 trio of Parsons, Denneulin and

Serving with SPA3, Lt Tadia Sondrmajer was the only Serbian pilot to fly combat missions over the Western Front. On 21 May 1918 he downed a German two-seater, but later that same day his aeroplane caught fire in the air and he came down badly burned (*August Blume collection via Jon Guttman*)

Chevannes shot down a two-seater over Montdidier. The 20th saw Parsons became an ace at the expense of a German two-seater, while Naudin of SPA26 downed a scout near Orvillers.

On the 21st, Lt Sondrmajer intercepted an enemy two-seater that was outrunning two other SPADs and sent it crashing near Montigny-le-Franc, killing Flg Johann Pöhlmann and Vfw Franz Mühlberger of *Schlachtstaffel* 30b. As Sondrmajer was returning from his second sortie of the day, however, his SPAD caught fire, and although he made it to earth, he was badly burned and spent the next four months in hospital. Promoted to captain after his release, he saw out the remaining months of the war in Serbian service, and afterward in the army of the new kingdom of Yugoslavia.

After a bout of bad weather, Baylies caught a German scout molesting a French artillery spotter on 28 May and shot it down near Courtemanch. He downed another enemy aeroplane the next day, while Bozon-Verduraz also claimed a victory. Dubonnet and Baylies teamed up to wreck another two-seater on 31 May, bringing the latter's total to 12.

This photograph of Lt Alfred Rougevin-Baville was taken whilst he was undergoing flying training at Cazeaux. On 20 April 1918 he shared in an aerial victory with Pillon. On 4 June he left SPA67 to take command of SPA99, and he was promoted to the rank of *capitaine* on 12 September (*SHAA B83.1479*)

After brief service in SPA73, Sgt Frank Leaman Baylies became SPA3's leading ace of 1918, scoring 12 victories before being killed in action on 17 June, probably by Ltn Wilhelm Leusch of *Jasta* 19

On 2 June, Coudouret and LFC squadronmate Sgt Robert B Hoeber shared in the destruction of a German fighter over Carlepont. This was the sixth for the 22-year-old Coudouret, who had scored single victories while serving in N57 and N102, and three more with N581 in Russia in 1917. An unidentified two-seater also fell victim to SPA103 pilot Adjutant Baux that same day.

Lt Rougevin-Baville, who had transferred from SPA67 to SPA3 on 3 May 1918, departed on 4 June to take command of SPA99. On 7 June GC12 returned to Hétomesnil. Naudin scored his third victory and SPA67's commander, Capitaine d'Indy, logged his first confirmed success on the 11th, but at noon that day SPA94's new commander from SPA3, Lt de la Rochefordière, was shot down in flames by two Fokker D VIIs near Méry Lataule and was probably credited to Ltn Kurt Hetze of *Jasta* 13. Dubonnet and Chevannes burned a balloon on the 13th.

On 17 June Baylies, 'borrowing' Risacher's SPAD because his own was suffering from engine trouble, was leading Dubonnet and Sgt François Macari on patrol when they spotted a higher formation of four rotary-engined aeroplanes that they assumed to be British Sopwiths. Baylies was climbing toward them when Dubonnet reported that Baylies' SPAD 'leaped upward and then swung over on one wing' as he realised his error and three Fokker Dr Is dived on him. Baylies looped onto the tail of one of his attackers, but a fourth Fokker that had been flying top cover for the other three pounced on his SPAD and shot it down in flames near Rollot. Macari disengaged from the ensuing fight, but Dubonnet's SPAD was riddled, and he just managed to coax his crippled machine over the lines before pancaking in French territory.

On 6 July a German aeroplane dropped a message in French lines, 'Pilot Baylies killed in combat. Buried with military honours'. He was probably the victim of Ltn Rudolf Rienau of *Jasta* 19, while Dubonnet was credited to Ltn Wilhelm Leusch of that unit. The loss of 'Jules' Baylies was almost as painful a blow to SPA3 in 1918 as Guynemer's had been in 1917. In 1927 the American ace's remains were reinterred at the *Memorial de l'Escadrille Lafayette* in the Parc Revue Villeneuve l'Étang, eight miles from the centre of Paris.

Adjutant Henri Prétre of SPA67 was flying a dawn patrol when he caught and shot down a German aircraft near Frétoy at 0545 hrs on 25 June. At 1600 hrs that same day, Fonck, just returned from a ceremony making him an *Officer de la Légion d'Honneur* at Dijon, dispatched a Halberstadt CL II, followed by two Fokker D VIIs in the next 30 minutes. Fonck struck again at 0810 hrs on the 27th, sending another Halberstadt CL II down in flames with just five rounds and, in spite of having to clear a gun jam, bringing down a second two-seater near Moreuil five minutes later. Adjutant Naudin and Lt Dombray downed a scout in flames over the Bois de Fay the next day, but on the 29th Cpl Jean Mandray of SPA103 also died in flames, probably the victim of Vfw Josef Schwendemann of *Jasta* 41.

The last day of June saw Capitaine d'Indy made a *Chevalier de la Légion d'Honneur*, and on 3 July Sous-Lt Bozon-Verduraz departed to succeed his late SPA3 squadronmate de la Rochfordière as commander of SPA94. He would lead the *escadrille* ably to the end of the war, and bring his own victory tally up to 11.

TO VICTORY

The first two weeks of July 1918 proved to be yet another calm before the last storm, as German forces prepared for their final bid to break though to Paris, although Naudin scored his fifth victory over Craonne on the 12th. Capitaine Raymond was slightly injured on 13 July when his SPAD XIII crashed upon returning from a patrol. Then, on the morning of the 15th, the group received urgent orders to return to the Champagne front – the Fourth Battle of the Champagne had begun with a thunderous artillery barrage, followed by a German attempt to force their way across the Marne.

SPA103 was the first to move to Trécon, supporting Général Henri Matais Berthelot's *Vème Armée*, on the 16th. Fonck, who had departed in the morning to stop in Paris to pick up some personal items and lunch for some comrades, was on his way to the new aerodrome when he spotted two German two-seaters, protected by six Fokkers, above Dormans. In spite of his cluttered cockpit, he circled around to a favourable position, then made a frontal diving attack, streaking past the escorts and firing at the two-seaters in quick succession, at ranges of 100 and 25 metres, respectively.

'I was a little worried because of the valises,' Fonck wrote. 'While watching my packages, I then made a little banking dive at full speed. Nothing budged in the cockpit – everything was fine. The Germans behind me were still 500 metres away, but they did not gain an inch, and I was heading in the direction of our lines. While turning around, I spotted two big black trails of smoke which told me that my bullets had hit

Lt Fonck poses beside his SPAD XIII 'VI', which he apparently flew for much of 1918. On 26 September he scored his second sextuple victory in a day, although the circumstances were more controversial than the first time (*SHAA B89.3679*)

home, and that my two-seaters had gone down in flames.' Fonck had become the first French airman since Guynemer to exceed 50 victories – and the only one other than he to do so.

SPA3 and SPA26 arrived at Trécon on 17 July, and in concert with SPA103 and GC11, they flew a grand total of 102 sorties that afternoon, including nine aerial combats and six balloon attacks. The day ended sadly for SPA103, however, when Adjutant Auguste Baux was shot down and killed near Cuchery by a Hannover CL IIIa of Fl. Abt. 295, crewed by Gefr Johann Baur and Ltn Georg von Hengl. Observer Hengl would end up with seven victories to his credit and Baur with six, the latter going on to gain more notoriety as Adolf Hitler's personal pilot.

By 18 July Germany's last bid for victory had ground to a complete halt, and the Allies launched a massive counteroffensive, pitting 45 infantry divisions against the 31 that the Germans had on the line. Général Charles Mangin's *Xème Armée* spearheaded the main French assault, supported on the right flank by the *VIème Armée* and by the *Véme* on the left, with Général Antoine Henri de Mitry's *IXéme Armée* in ready reserve. Fonck downed two Fokkers within ten minutes that morning, tying Guynemer's score. The following morning saw him surpass Guynemer by sending two Fokker D VIIs down in flames in two minutes, to which he added a two-seater at 1555 that afternoon.

Although Fonck's conceited manner kept him from gaining the affection that his colleagues still reserved for the late Guynemer, his skill could not be denied, and squadronmate Sgt Jean Laffray testified that Fonck did set an inspiring example among SPA103 pilots. A case in point occurred at 1800 hrs on 21 July, when Adjutant Loup and Sgt Drouillh again teamed up to drive a Fokker crashing to earth, and probably downed another.

Sgt Lenoir of SPA103 was wounded in the foot during the same combat, however, and SPA26 lost Cpl François Hugues – both possibly victims of *Jasta* 8, which credited victories to Vfw Wilhelm Anton Seitz,

Although Fonck was far from universally liked in GC12, Sgt Jean Laffray was one of several SPA103 members who respected and admired him for his leadership by example (*Jon Guttman*)

Capitaine Joseph Battle poses before a captured Friedrichshafen G III bomber. Already victor over one enemy aeroplane while serving in N77, Battle added three more to his score between July and August 1918 while commanding SPA103 (*SHAA B85.2122*)

Uffz Rudolf Francke and Vfw Hoppe at 1925 hrs German time, without recording any casualties.

During the dawn patrol on 22 July, Sous-Lt Pendaries became an ace when he and Adjutant Marcel Jaubert of SPA67 sent a two-seater down to crash near Ville-en-Tardenois at 0545 hrs. Capitaine Battle of SPA103 burned a balloon north of Epoye at 0700 hrs, but Fonck's only victory of the day went unconfirmed – his 43rd 'probable' thus far.

A three-day stretch of poor weather allowed GC12 to move 25 kilometres south to Herbisse, but by 29 July all four *escadrilles* had returned to Hétomesnil in preparation for the offensive that Gen Henry Rawlinson's Fourth Army was about to commence against the German salient around Amiens, supported on the right flank by Debeney's Iére *Armée*.

While waiting for the British push to begin, Naudin, Adjutant Justin Usse and Sgt Aimé Vincent of SPA26 burned a balloon at Lançon on 31 July. It was Naudin's sixth, and final, victory. Fonck downed a two-seater east of the Bois d'Hangard the next day, while Raymond, recovered from his injuries, returned to assume command of SPA3.

The British launched their Amiens offensive on 8 August, which Gen Erich Ludendorf would subsequently call the 'Black Day for the German Army'. Activity was as heavy in the air as on the ground, but GC12 did not confirm a victory until 9 August, when Risacher of SPA3 bested a German fighter over Bouchoir, and Battle of SPA103 destroyed another near Etelfay, probably killing Ltn Egon Patzer of *Jasta* 36. SPA26 got into a scrap over Grevillers at 2015 hrs on 11 August, during which Sgt Armand Lebroussard downed a German fighter and Sous-Lt Puget and Sgt Jean Pelletier drove another down in flames.

'On 14 August 1918 I succeeded in shooting down three Boches within ten seconds,' Fonck wrote, adding, 'This was my record as far as speed was concerned. They came toward me following each other at 50-metre intervals. Upon crossing them, I cut loose a burst at each one, and each time my bullets hit their target. They fell near the city of Roye and ended up by burning on the ground, separated by less than 100 metres. These were my 58th, 59th and 60th official Boches.'

Dubonnet shared in the destruction of two two-seaters with the commanders of two neighbouring squadrons on the 16th – one with Capitaine Battle of SPA103 and the other with SPA26's Capitaine de Sevin – bringing his total to six. Dubonnet, who became a *Chevalier de la Légion d'Honneur* in January 1936, served in *Groupe de Chasse* I/2 during World War 2, and died on 20 January 1980. Sous-Lt Schmitter and Adjutant Baron of SPA103 downed another two-seater near St Mard on 16 August, but SPA3 lost Sous-Lt Jean Edouard Caël.

A Parisian who had formerly served in MF25, MF16, MF2 and C56, before training in fighters, Caël had joined N102 on 20 September 1916 and scored three victories with that unit before transferring to SPA3 on 15 June 1918. During the fight on 16 August, the 22-year-old Caël had helped a beleaguered British aeroplane disengage from several Fokkers, but his own SPAD XIII (S4848) was brought down by Oblt Ernst Udet,

Louis Risacher poses beside his Blériot-built SPAD XIII. On 9 August Lt Risacher scored his second confirmed victory, but eight days later he was transferred to SPA159, where he raised his total to five (*Louis Risacher album via Jon Guttman*)

who by that time was *Staffelführer* of *Jasta* 4 of the late Red Baron's 'Circus'. On 24 January 1919 Caël, who had already earned the *Croix de Guerre* with four palms and the *Belgian Croix de Guerre* before becoming a PoW, was made a *Chevalier de la Légion d'Honneur*.

On the 17th, MdL Patay of SPA26 was shot down in SPAD VII S3257 by Uffz Vahldieck of *Jasta* 50. That same day, Sous-Lt Risacher left SPA3 to serve as executive officer of SPA159, with which unit he would eventually achieve acedom with three more victories. Capitaine d'Indy of SPA67 collaborated with MdL Hubert Lambotte of SPA26 to bring down a two-seater near Armancourt on 20 August, its crew being taken prisoner.

On 22 August GC12 added a fifth *escadrille* to its roster when SPA167 was formed with 12 SPAD XIIIs and six SPAD VIIs. Its commander, Bernard Henri Barny de Romanet, was born in Saint Maurice de Sathonay on 28 January 1894. Joining the infantry in October 1913, he entered aviation in July 1915 as an observer with C51, and received his pilot's brevet on 5 January 1916. After further service in C51, Romanet retrained as a fighter pilot and returned to combat with N37, rising to the rank of lieutenant by June 1918 and scoring his tenth victory on the very day he was assigned to his new command.

Romanet's second-in-command was Sous-Lt Victor Espéron de Tremblay, and his other officers included a cadre of experienced veterans, including former N3 member Joseph Guiguet. After his grievous injuries of 23 May 1917, Guiguet had emerged from convalescence with one leg

Victor over three enemy aeroplanes while in SPA102 before joining SPA3, Sous-Lt Jean Edouard Caël was made a *Chevalier de la Légion d'Honneur* for his efforts to protect a beleaguered British aeroplane on 16 August 1918, until he was brought down and taken prisoner by Oblt Ernst Udet of *Jasta* 4 (*SHAA B91.4806*)

five centimetres shorter than the other, requiring him to get about on the ground with the aid of a walking stick. In spite of that, Guiguet felt that by adjusting the rudder bar he could still fly an aeroplane well enough to avenge the deaths of Dorme and his other comrades.

On 30 November 1917 his sous-lieutenant's commission became permanent, and he subsequently convinced his superiors to reassign him to frontline duty. Just before returning to combat, however, he decided to marry Lucienne Vachon, whom he had met at Le Bourget three years earlier. They were married at Corbelin on 8 June 1918, and about two months later, on 19 August, Guiguet arrived at the *Groupe des Division d'Entrainement*. After familiarising himself with the SPAD XIII, he was assigned in September to SPA167, where the younger pilots came to refer to him affectionately by a sobriquet once held by his late friend from the glory day at N3 – *'Père'* Guiguet.

Another 'old hand' who Romanet habitually chose as his wingman on patrols was Sous-Lt François Dumas. Nicknamed 'Gédéon' by his comrades – including Guiguet, whom he had met when they underwent flight training together at Pau – Dumas had since flown alongside Romanet in C51, before switching to fighters and serving in N57, with which unit he was credited with two victories.

SPA67 lost Cpl Gaston Sachet on the 22nd when he fatally crash-landed his SPAD VII, but Usse of SPA26 scored his second victory on 25 August, and on the 29th Parsons of SPA3 added a Fokker D VII to his score.

SPA3 lost its commander again on 3 September when Capitaine Raymond was hospitalised with the dreaded 'Spanish flu', to which he would fatally succumb on 4 October. Lt Aimé Grasset, a 29-year-old veteran pilot and *Chevalier de la Légion d'Honneur*, was transferred from SPA150 to take over command of SPA3. On 8 September, with the

Joseph Guiguet takes the wheel of a Hispano Suiza Torpedo donated to N3 by the company – for which it was rewarded with numerous photos of its heroes posing therein! After being wounded on 23 May 1917, Guiguet returned to GC12 as a member of SPA167, with which he finally achieved acedom on 24 October 1918 (*SHAA B86.1182*)

British offensive continuing to go well, GC12 began moving to Lisle-en-Barrois to help support the American Expeditionary Force's first offensive of the war, at St Mihiel. The Storks played only a peripheral role in the action, however, with no confirmed victories and only one casualty – Adjutant Vincent of SPA26, wounded on 14 September. The Americans eliminated the German salient at St Mihiel on the 18th, and on the same day GC12 began moving to La Noblette, in preparation for a joint Franco-American advance in, and adjacent to, the Bois d'Argonne.

Although the start of the Meuse–Argonne offensive would soon stall in the face of well-prepared and stubborn German resistance on the ground on 26 September, the day would be a memorable one for GC12. Adjutant-Chef Naudin started things off by probably downing a two-seater at 1015 hrs. Fonck sent two Fokker D VIIs crashing near Sommepy at 1145 hrs, followed at 1210 hrs by a Halberstadt two-seater over Perthes-les-Hurlus, killing Uffz Richard Scholl and Ltn d R Eugen Anderer of Fl. Abt. (A) 233.

The 26th also saw SPA167 embark on its first combat sortie. 'Romanet,' wrote Guiguet, 'with Dumas, his habitual wingman, had sort of thrown me into the bath by incorporating me into their patrol, for my first sortie into that infernal circus from which I had been away for such a long time. The dogfights became, particularly between single-seaters, real acrobatic tourneys.' Indeed, the first such melée occurred on that very flight, when the three Frenchmen encountered a formation of Fokkers. Romanet made a probable claim over a Fokker, but his subsequent report of the engagement indicated what he viewed as being of greater importance. 'The pilots all returned without one bullet in their aeroplanes,' he wrote. 'Good start – we are all happy.'

At 1800 hrs Parsons and Denneulin of SPA3 teamed up with Sous-Lt Pendaries of SPA67 to destroy a two-seater south of Tahure. Long after the war, Parsons said of Denneulin;

'He was my guardian angel. He became one of the Air France's top pilots, and in 1928 I had the pleasure of flying with him over our old hunting ground on a regular Paris–London flight. It was a great source of personal tragedy for me that a short time later I received notice of his death from pneumonia.'

Fonck was leading a patrol with three other SPA103 pilots when he spotted eight Fokkers over St Souplet at 1805 hrs. 'I awaited the attack confidently, and would have willingly provoked it when a SPAD came in unexpectedly to lend a hand,' Fonck wrote. 'I immediately recognised Capitaine de Sevin and the "Storks" of the 26th.'

The French attacked, but the Germans gave Fonck one of the most difficult fights of his career. Adjutant Brugère downed a Fokker, but was attacked by two others, one of which Fonck claimed to have shot down in the process of rescuing him. 'During this time,' Fonck added, 'Capitaine de Sevin was going through a very risky acrobatic manoeuvre in order to shake off a Boche who had come to grips with him, and who seemed to me to be a rather bold devil. Only the captain's skill as a pilot permitted him to escape, for his motor had conked out and he was pursued to within 100 metres from the ground.'

Five Albatros two-seaters entered the melée, and Fonck downed two of them as well. 'Two others owed their skins to a jamming of my machine gun,' he stated, 'and despite the cold, which perpetually reigns in high

113

altitude, I must confess I felt drenched with perspiration upon returning to the field.'

For the second time in the war, Fonck had scored six victories in one day. British Sopwith Camel aces John Trollope and Henry Woollett, and German Fokker D VII *Kanone* Franz Büchner had equalled his feat, but only Fonck had done it twice. One of those victories was also claimed by de Sevin, but credited only to Fonck, who, not having crash-landed, had been able to submit his claim first. De Sevin's SPAD, which came down in French lines, was one of two credited to Ltn d R Karl Maletsky of *Jasta* 50, but another of the Germans, Vzfw Karl Weinmann, also descended in French lines and was taken prisoner.

During a ground attack mission by SPA26 on the 29th, ground fire seriously wounded Naudin in the foot and disabled the SPAD of MdL Robert Brillaut, who nevertheless force-landed unhurt behind Allied lines. Aside from the intense action of the 26th, September had been relatively unproductive for the Storks, but they would make up for it in October by scoring 31 victories – nearly a third of which would be credited to SPA167, which had not commenced combat operations until late in the previous month.

Cpl Jean de Lombardon got the carnage started on 1 October when he and Romanet went after a German reconnaissance aeroplane. Romanet suffered a gun jam, but Lombardon pressed home the attack and sent the

Fonck of SPA103 (left) turns to the camera beside Lt Gustave Lagache of SPA3 and Lt Bernard Barny de Romanet, commander of GC12's fifth *escadrille*, SPA167 (*SHAA B88.3570*)

enemy aeroplane crashing near Bétheniville at 1045 hrs for SPA167's first confirmed success. At 1245 hrs Adjutant Drouillh and Sgt Sansom of SPA103 claimed two Fokkers northwest of Sommepy, one of which was confirmed. At 1510 hrs Parsons attacked an artillery spotting aeroplane north of Sommpy, and after a fight lasting less than 30 seconds in which he fired only five or six rounds, he sent it spinning down to crash, killing Ltn Hermann Kottwitz and Viktor Neumann of Fl. Abt. 239. That brought the former *Lafayette Escadrille* pilot's score to eight.

During the post-war years, Parsons worked as an agent for the Federal Bureau of Investigation, and as a writer or advisor on several aviation films. He also wrote for pulp magazines, published a book on his wartime experiences and wrote and narrated a 15-minute radio series, *Heroes of the Lafayette*. In 1940, Parsons joined the US Navy as a lieutenant commander, served in the Solomon Islands and rose to the rank of rear admiral by the end of World War 2. After receiving a rather overdue *Légion d'Honneur* in 1962, Edwin Parsons died on 2 May 1968 and is buried at Arlington National Cemetery.

The next day saw the return to combat of one of SPA26's earliest heroes, Sous-Lt Roland Garros. Already a renowned pre-war aviator who had escaped from German internment soon after the war began, Garros had installed steel deflectors on the propeller of his Morane Saulnier L parasol to score three victories in April 1915, but came down in German lines on the 18th and was taken prisoner. After several failed attempts, he finally escaped from the Germans for the second time on 14 February 1918, and after rehabilitation and retraining, he was assigned to SPA103 on 20 August, transferring to SPA26 three days later. Aggressive as ever, he claimed two Fokker D VIIs on 2 October, one of which was confirmed for his fourth victory. Speculation was rife that he would soon attain his long-overdue status as an ace.

Another welter of activity on 3 October began with Romanet and Lombardon sending a Fokker D VII to crash near Mont Blanc, where they

On 23 August 1918 one of *escadrille* 26's earliest heroes returned in the person of Lt Roland Garros, seen in the middle (wearing the beret) beside a Nieuport 28. Captured after downing three German aircraft in April 1915, he finally escaped on 14 February 1918. On 2 October he was credited with a Fokker D VII for his fourth victory, and speculation was rife that he would soon attain long-overdue ace status (*SHAA B87.1456*)

Garros boards his Blériot-built SPAD XIII S15409 of SPA26. On 5 October 1918 he was killed in action, probably downed by Ltn d R Hermann Habich of *Jasta* 49 (*Musée de l'Air et de l'Espace, BA26287*)

observed it burning on the ground at 1010 hrs. That afternoon SPA26 attacked 14 Fokkers of *Jasta* 60 that had just burned a balloon of the *67e Compagnie d'Aérostiers* east of Somme-Py, which was credited to Ltn Karl Ritscherle. In the course of the dogfight Sgt Brillaut was credited with a Fokker – whose pilot apparently survived – but suffered a flesh wound in the back. In a third engagement at 1450 hrs, Lt Robert le Petit of SPA67 drove another Fokker down between Moronvillers and Dontrien.

One day after Georges Raymond's death from influenza, GC12 mourned another grievous loss on 5 October, when Garros went missing in SPAD XIII S15409 after last having been seen battling seven Fokkers southwest of Vouziers. World War 1's first fighter pilot was probably killed by Ltn d R Hermann Habich of *Jasta* 49, who claimed a SPAD XIII near Somme-Py. Lt Dombray and MdL Lambotte sought to avenge

Garros by driving down two-seaters, but neither were confirmed. Fonck was credited with crashing a two-seater and a Fokker that day, however, as well as two 'probables'.

After another bout of poor weather, Romanet sent a two-seater crashing south of Bignicourt at 0700 hrs on 10 October, which was witnessed by the 21ème and 55ème Compagnies Aérostiers. SPA167's commander downed another in concert with 'Gédéon' Dumas on the 14th, bringing the latter's score up to three. On the 16th, GC12 acquired a sixth squadron when SPA173 was formed under Lt Jacques Allez, a 24-year-old former cuirassier and fighter pilot with SPA65.

Aerial activity intensified at 1430 hrs on 18 October, with Lombardon probably downing a two-seater, while Romanet and Dumas claimed two Fokkers over Givry-sur-Aisne, one of which was confirmed. Drouillh and Sansom downed another Fokker in flames at 1625 hrs. When the next opportunities for success arose on the 23rd, SPA167 was again in the forefront, Romanet and Sous-Lt Marcel Lechavalier destroying a two-

Late in the war a few SPAD XVIIs made their way into service with GC12, although they fell disappointingly short of expectations as improvements over the SPAD XIII. One went to SPA103 and was flown by Capitaine René Fonck (*SHAA B81.1397*)

seater south of Le Chesne at 1215 hrs, and Romanet eliminating a Fokker near Attigny at 1625 hrs.

Xavier de Sevin scored his 12th, and final, victory at 1400 hrs on 24 October. One hour later Romanet and Guiguet intercepted an enemy two-seater north of Attigny, and after several firing passes sent it spinning down. Three days later ground witnesses confirmed its crash, bringing Guiguet into the ace category at long last.

SPA26 stole the limelight on 28 October, with German fighters falling victim to Adjutant Usse, Lt Letourneau and Sgt René Dard between 1530 and 1545 hrs. On that same day Lt Grasset was reassigned to the *Centre d'Instruction de l'aviation de Chasse et de Bombardment*, and Lt Dombray of SPA26 took his place as SPA3's last wartime commander.

Aspirant Emile Villard and Sgt Lombardon of SPA167 shot down a two-seater north of Attigny at 1030 hrs on 29 October, while Pendaries downed a two-seater between Amancourt and Lamtez at 1317 hrs, bringing his score to seven, and Romanet crashed a two-seater south of the Bois de Loges at 1500 hrs for his 18th, and final, confirmed success.

Good, clear weather on the 30th resulted in a patrol from SPA103 sending a balloon down in flames over Quatre-Champs at 0810 hrs, as well as a two-seater falling to Sgt Brière of SPA3 and another to Sous-Lt de Tascher and MdL Marcel Plessis of SPA26.

Guiguet, patrolling since morning, encountered a two-seater near Grandpré and engaged it in a running fight that took them 20 kilometres to the east and down to an altitude of 6000 metres before he finally sent it crashing to the ground near Dun-sur-Meuse. Due to the confusion of fighting in the area, Guiguet was unable to find enough witnesses to confirm his success.

Fonck also returned to action with his usual deadly aplomb that afternoon, sending a two-seater down in flames near Falaise at 1525 hrs and picking off two fighters between Semay and Terron 15 minutes later. He shot the wings off a two-seater north of Vouziers at 1120 hrs the next day, and dispatched an enemy fighter east of the town 15 minutes later.

GC12 began moving to Hauviné, 25 kilometres north-northeast of Reims, on 1 November. Five patrols were flown that morning, but the only confirmed claims for the day were from SPA103 – a Halberstadt crashed

This photograph shows GC12 members late in the war, including Cpl André Henon of SPA167 (left), Brigadier Max Ouvrard de Linière of SPA67 (fourth from left), Adjutant Gilbert Loup of SPA103 (sixth from left), MdL Henri Alibert of SPA67 (eighth from left) and Sgt George McCall of SPA103 (right). An LFC volunteer from Pennsylvania, McCall had served in *escadrilles* N23, SPA48 and C30 before joining SPA103 on 24 October 1918 (*SHAA B85.2126*)

east of Vouziers at 1410 hrs, bringing Fonck's total to 75, and making him the Allied ace of aces. Another enemy aeroplane was also downed that day by Sgt Schmitter and MdL Gui. Sgt Albert Beroulle of SPA26 went missing on the morning of 4 November, and that same day Capitaine Battle transferred out of SPA103 and Capitaine Dupuy took command of that *escadrille*, as well as the group overall. Poor weather limited further sorties by GC12 until 1100 hrs on 11 November 1918, when word of the signing of the Armistice brought an end to hostilities right across the front. World War 1 was over.

Since its formation on 1 November 1916, GC12 had been credited with a grand total of 286 aircraft and five balloons destroyed, for the loss of 17 men killed in action, 16 missing in action, six taken prisoner (counting Louis Paoli's temporary internment in the Netherlands), 29 wounded in action (two mortally), eight killed in accidents and ten injured in accidents, one of whom later died of his injuries. The top-scoring French *escadrille* of the war was SPA3, with a wartime total of 175 victories, of which 106 aeroplanes and one balloon were confirmed to it during its time as the heart of GC12.

During GC12's existence, SPA26 was credited with 31 aircraft, SPA67 downed 14 aeroplanes, SPA73 accounted for 20 aeroplanes and one balloon and R46 gained two of its wartime total of 37 victories during its brief attachment to the group. SPA103's tally of 103 aeroplanes and three balloons with GC12 – and 111 overall – was second only to SPA3's in the French air service. Equally remarkable was the fact that 73 of those victories had been scored by one man.

With a total of 75 confirmed victories – and 52 unconfirmed – René Fonck was the undisputed Allied ace of aces, yet he never received the public adulation that went to Georges Guynemer or Charles Nungesser. In 1926 he tried to fly the Atlantic Ocean from New York to Paris, but his overloaded Sikorsky S 35 crashed on take-off, killing two of its four-man crew. He served as inspector of France's fighter force prior to 1940, but after World War 2 he was accused of collaborating with the Germans, though he was never brought to trial. Fonck was 59 when he died in Paris on 18 June 1953, an unrequited seeker of glory who could easily have stood on the record of his deeds, if only he had seen fit to do so.

Brigadier René Ouvrard de Linière, one of three brothers who flew in GC12, poses beside his SPAD XIII of SPA103 probably after the armistice (*SHAA B85.218*)

SPA173 did not enter combat in time to add to GC12's laurels, but SPA167 had, scoring an impressive ten victories in October 1918 and, even more remarkably, doing so without suffering a single combat casualty. Alas, it commander and leading ace, Bernard Barny de Romanet, was killed in a post-war flying accident on 23 September 1921.

Although GC12's collective total of victories was 291, counting the overall wartime successes of its component *escadrilles* in and out of the group would produce a total of 411 aeroplanes and 11 balloons. In addition to the pantheon of aces it produced, 13 members of GC12 went on to command other squadrons or larger formations, including Americans C Maury Jones as leader of the 28th Aero Squadron and Charles Biddle with the 13th Aero Squadron and 4th Pursuit Group.

After GC12 performed post-war duty with the Army of Occupation in Germany, the French air service underwent a reorganisation, during which SPA3, SPA26 and SPA103 were grouped within the *2e Régiment de Chasse Strasbourg*, commanded by Commandant Félix Brocard, on 31 December 1919. The squadrons of GC12, and their stork insignias, were to live on under other designations through World War 2. *Groupe de Chasse* I/2, equipped with Morane Saulnier MS406 fighters, retained the SPA3 and SPA103 traditions, destroying 25 German aircraft by 25 June

Louis Risacher, formerly of SPA3 and SPA159, revisits an old acquaintance – the SPAD XIII at the *Musée de l'Air et de l'Espace* during the last international reunion of World War 1 aces, held in November 1981 (*Jon Guttman*)

Old enemies compare notes as former Richthofen 'Circus' ace Alois Heldmann of *Jasta* 10 (15 victories) describes an aerial combat to former *Cigogne* Louis Risacher at the international World War 1 aces' reunion in November 1981 (*Jon Guttman*)

1940, and then carrying on in North Africa until the Allied invasion in November 1942, when it became No 329 'Free French' Sqn, RAF. GCI/5, retaining the stork on a pennant of SPA67, was France's highest-scoring unit by 25 June 1940, with 117 accredited victories, although ironically its fighters were American-supplied Curtiss Hawk 75As.

After World War 2, the resurrected GCI/2 'Cigognes' served in Indochina between 30 June 1946 and 1 October 1954. As of this writing the group, equipped with Dassault Mirage 2000C fighters, currently operates from Dijon-Longvic, ready, if the need ever arises, to uphold the traditions established by its illustrious World War 1 forebears.

Another survivor – Guynemer's first 180-hp SPAD VII, S254, has been restored and can still be seen on display at the *Musée de l'Air et de l'Espace* at Le Bourget (*Jon Guttman*)

APPENDICES

APPENDIX 1

ACES WHO FLEW IN GC12

Name	Escadrille	Victories with GC12	Overall
René Fonck	SPA103	73	75
Georges Guynemer	N3	35	53
Armand Pinsard	N26	1	27
René Dorme	N3	7	23
Claude Haegelen	N103	2	22
Alfred Heurtaux	N3	11	21
Albert Deullin	N3, N73	12	20
Bernard Barny de Romanet	SPA167	8	18
Frank Leaman Baylies	SPA73, SPA3	12	12
Xavier de Sevin	SPA26	5	12
Benjamin Bozon-Verduraz	SPA3	8	11
Mathieu Tenant de la Tour	N3, SPA26	2	9
Edwin Charles Parsons	SPA3	7	8
Armand Pillon	N67	2	8
Charles John Biddle	SPA73	1	8
Alfred Auger	N3	5	7
Pierre Pendaries	SPA67	4	7
François Battesti	N73	3	7
André Dubonnet	SPA3	6	6
Gustave Naudin	SPA26	6	6
Georges Raymond	SPA3	5	6
Constant Soulier	N26	4	6
Louis Coudouret	SPA103	1	6
Joseph Henri Guiguet	N3, SPA167	4	5
Louis Risacher	SPA3	2	5
Ivan Orlov	N3	1	5

1

Nieuport 17 N1720 of Adjutant René Dorme, N3, Cachy, November 1916

'Père' Dorme is known to have flown Nieuport 17 N1720 from 3 September to 20 December 1916, when he was wounded. By that time he had used it to add eight German aircraft to his score, including two since N3 had been incorporated into GC12, on 16 November and 4 December. After returning to N3, Dorme continued to fly N1720 until the end of January 1917. This Nieuport had a clear cellon panel in the upper centre section to improve upward pilot visibility, with its number repeated on the upper right wing and Dorme's green Cross of Lorraine on the upper fuselage decking.

2

Nieuport 17 N2007 of Adjutant Joseph Henri Guiguet, N3, Cachy, December 1916

First delivered to N3 on 16 October 1916, Nieuport 17 N2007 had been flown by Lt Maxime Benois (Commandant Félix Brocard's assistant on the GC12 staff) until Guiguet took it over on 16 November and applied his number '8' and trademark legend *'P'tit Jo II'*. Already credited with a balloon on 22 May 1916 prior to joining N3, Guiguet used N2007 to shot down German two-seaters on 15 and 20 December, as well as a 'probable' on 5 January 1917. As with Dorme's aeroplane, it had a clear cellon panel in the upper wing centre section and the numeral on the right upper wing.

3

SPAD VII S113 of Lt Alfred Heurtaux, N3, Cachy, autumn 1916

A red stork and numeral, and nothing else, appeared on Heurtaux's SPAD. By the time GC12 was formed, he had downed ten opponents, including German ace Ltn Kurt Wintgens on 25 September 1916. Two days after the group's formation, he shot down an Aviatik, and brought his total to 21 by 4 May 1917.

4

SPAD VII S392 of Sous-Lt René Dorme, N3, Bonnemaison, spring 1917

After scoring one victory in SPAD VII S314, Dorme picked up S392 at Buc on 28 March 1917. This featured a wide radiator aperture and the high-compression 180-hp Hispano Suiza 8Ab engine. On 24 April Dorme wrote to Louis Béchereau, 'My supercompression aircraft, which is well tuned, gives me absolute confidence'. Christened simply *'Père Dorme'*, S392 was photographed with both the standard windscreen and one that was cut down for easier cockpit access from the left. There was no number on the upper wing. Dorme scored his last six victories in this plane, but was also killed in it on 25 May 1917, as the fifth victory for Ltn Heinrich Kroll of *Jasta* 9.

5

SPAD VII S1422 of Sous-Lt Georges Raymond, Bonnemaison, N3, July 1917

All of Raymond's Nieuports and SPADs bore the numeral '9' and the legend *'Ma Ninon'*. S1422 was one of at least two SPAD VIIs to bear those markings, and may have been used when he scored his third victory on 16 August 1917. Born in Lyon on 19 June 1887, Georges Raymond began his wartime career in the cavalry, later switching to aviation and joining N3 in May 1916. Although he was a ubiquitous presence, and became a *Chevalier de la Legion d'Honneur* in May 1918, his entry into *les Cigognes'* ace roster was a protracted affair, beginning on 25 September 1916 and ending with his fifth victory on 20 February 1918. He commanded SPA3 from 2 November 1917 through to 4 October 1918, when he died of pneumonia.

6

SPAD VII S420 of Adjutant René Guillaumot, N3, Bonnemaison, July 1917

Born in Paris in 1894, Guillaumot entered aviation in 1915 and flew in MF1, before joining N3 on 5 October 1916. He was cited four times, although his only victories were probables. His post-war flying took him to Syria and Indochina, before he returned to France as a test pilot. Guillaumot was killed while test-flying a Nieuport Delage 42 at Villacoublay on 11 August 1927.

7

SPAD VII S1416 of Capitaine Alfred Victor Constantin Robert Auger, N3, Bonnemaison, July 1917

Boasting a 180-hp Hispano Suiza engine, S1416 was flown by Capitaine Auger, who apparently changed numbers from '7' to '6' after André Chainat left N3. In addition to the tricolour band and legend *'Je'*, Auger adorned his fighter with artwork depicting a four-leaf clover and a German speared on the tip of his stork's beak. He may have used this aeroplane to score his sixth and seventh victories in June 1917, but Sgt Georges Silberstein was killed while 'borrowing' it for a training flight on 6 July – the same day he had joined the *escadrille*. Auger was mortally wounded in combat soon after, on 28 July 1917. He managed to land his SPAD in French lines before he died, and the soldiers who arrived on the scene found that he had flown his last mission with the national flag draped around his body.

8

SPAD VII S1639 of Sous-Lt Henri Rabatel, N3, St Pol-sur-Mer, August 1917

One of many victims of GC12's sojourn at St Pol-sur-Mer, near Dunkirk, Sous-Lt Rabatel had been credited with two victories when he was brought down on 16 August 1917 by Obflgmstr Kurt Schönfelder, a naval pilot assigned to *Jasta* 7, and taken prisoner.

9

SPAD XII S382 of Capitaine Georges Guynemer, N3, St Pol-sur-Mer, July 1917

The first operational SPAD XII arrived at N3 for frontline evaluation in early July 1917, and Guynemer used his 37 mm cannon-armed *'avion magique'* to score victories on 27 and 28 July, as well as a double victory on 17 August.

10

SPAD XIII S504 of Capitaine Georges Guynemer, N3, St Pol-sur-Mer, September 1917

The livery of Guynemer's SPAD XIII included a black command pennant on the fuselage upper decking, an unusual variation on the tricolour band and a dark (possibly black) 'X' on the upper wing centre section, the significance of which is unknown. He received S504 in late July and used it to score his 53rd victory on 20 August 1917, but he went missing in the scout on 11 September.

11
SPAD XIII (serial unknown) of MdL Edmond Moulines, SPA3, Maisonneuve, January 1918
MdL Edouard Moulines' early model SPAD XIII was unusual, but not unique, in having its numeral on the upper left wing, rather than the right. One of the 'team players' who was as important to any squadron as the leaders and aces, Moulines was credited with assisting Lt Benjamin Bozon-Verduraz and Sgt Louis Risacher in the destruction of German aircraft on 15 and 16 May 1918.

12
SPAD XIII (serial unknown) of Lt Benjamin Bozon-Verduraz, SPA3, Hétomesnil, May 1918
Normally flown by Bozon-Verduraz, Blériot-built SPAD XIII '16' *Mon Lion* was 'borrowed' by Sgt Frank L Baylies – a close friend of both Bozon-Verduraz's and Louis Risacher's – when he scored his fifth victory on 19 May 1918. Relying more on his fearlessness and a strategy of closing to point-blank range to compensate for his lack of flying finesse and marksmanship, Bozon-Verduraz scored five victories with SPA3 and another three as commander of SPA94.

13
SPAD XIII (serial unknown) of Lt Tadia Sondrmajer, SPA3, Hétomesnil, May 1918
The only Serbian pilot to see combat over the Western Front, Tadia Sondrmajer added a two-seater to SPA3's account on 21 May 1918, but later that same day his aeroplane caught fire in the air, and although he survived, he was too badly burned to return to frontline flying with GC12.

14
SPAD XIII (serial unknown) of Sgt André Dubonnet, SPA3, Sacy-le-Grand, June 1918
Joining SPA3 on 29 April 1918, Dubonnet gained notoriety for more than just the cheer he could supply from his wine-making family, being credited with six victories.

15
SPAD XIII (serial unknown) of Sous-Lt Edwin C Parsons, SPA3, Ferme de la Noblette, October 1918
A mercenary adventurer with previous flying experience with Pancho Villa's Mexican revolutionaries, 'Ted' Parsons scored his first victory with N124 'Lafayette' before joining SPA3 in preference to transferring to the US Army Air Service. Reported to have flown '4 'as his regular aeroplane, he raised his tally to eight by the end of October 1918, and subsequently served in the US Navy during World War 2.

16
Nieuport 17 (serial unknown) of MdL Constant Soulier, N26, Cachy, January 1917
Based on a rather poor photograph, this Nieuport would still have had N26's original torch insignia on its fuselage sides and apparently had a tricolour cockade applied to its *cône de pénétration*. Soulier suffered a landing accident in this machine on 14 January 1917.

17
SPAD VII (serial unknown) of MdL Constant Soulier, N26, Bonne-Maison, spring 1917
Soulier's later SPAD VII apparently bore the red number '6', as well as N26's variant of the stork, as adopted throughout GC12. As a final personal touch, the Soulier seems to have had the cowling of his fighting scout painted blue.

18
SPAD VII (serial unknown) of Capitaine Kiyotake Shigeno, N26, Bonnemaison, July 1917
Already a *Chevalier de la Légion d'Honneur* with V24, Baron Shigeno was credited with at least two victories while serving in N26. In addition to standard N26 livery, his SPAD bore the legend *Wakadori*, in partial reference to his deceased wife Wakako (*'dori'* means bird in Japanese), below the cockpit. The red number '3' also appeared on the upper right wing, and a green four-leaf clover adorned the fuselage upper decking. On 9 August 1917 Shigeno was severely wounded in combat, possibly by Ltn zur See Gotthard von Sachsenberg of *Marine Feld Jasta* 1.

19
SPAD VII (serial unknown) of Sous-Lt André Dezarrois, N26, St Pol-sur-Mer, August 1917
Another of GC12's casualties during its fateful stint in the Dunkirk area, Sous-Lt Dezarrois was wounded in this aeroplane on 21 August 1917.

20
SPAD XIII (serial unknown) of Capitaine Joseph Marie Xavier de Sevin, SPA26, Ferme de la Noblette, September 1918
Xavier de Sevin had already claimed six victories with N12 and been made a *Chévalier de la Légion d'Honneur* prior to assuming command of SPA26 on 25 December 1917. This may explain why he indulged in a personal motif – a rose in a hunting horn, rather than the number '1' – to identify his SPAD XIII. De Sevin brought his wartime total to 12 on 24 October 1918.

21
SPAD XIII S15409 of Sous-Lt Roland Garros, SPA26, Ferme de la Noblette, October 1918
One of the great pre-war pioneer aviators, Garros became an innovator in fighter tactics when he used steel wedges on the propeller of a modified Morane Saulnier L parasol monoplane, allowing him to forward-fire a machine gun and down three enemy aeroplanes before going down in German lines on 18 April 1915. After escaping on 14 February 1918, he rejoined his old *escadrille*, SPA26, in August, flying Blériot-built SPAD XIII S15409 to vanquish a Fokker D VII for his fourth victory on 2 October. Garros, however, never quite 'made ace' before being killed in the same aeroplane three days later, probably being shot down by Ltn d R Hermann Habich of *Jasta* 49.

22

SPAD XIII (serial unknown) of Capitaine Marie Jacques d'Indy, SPA67, Hétomesnil, spring 1918

Born at Villain on 20 May 1888, Marie Jacques d'Indy entered military service in 1908 and served in cavalry units and the *Chasseurs d'Afrique* until 21 July 1915, when he transferred to aviation. Promoted to *capitaine* when he took command of N67 on 27 July 1917, d'Indy led the squadron until the Armistice. He scored his first aerial victory on 11 June 1918, was made a *Chevalier de la Légion d'Honneur* on 30 August and shared in bringing down a German two-seater in Allied lines on 20 August.

23

SPAD VII S401 of Lt Albert Deullin, N73, Bergues, July 1917

Lt Deullin was probably flying S401 when he scored his 17th victory on 21 July 1917. He was subsequently wounded in the aeroplane at 0900 hrs on 28 July 1917 – a bad day for GC12 commanders, since N3's leader, seven-victory ace Capitaine Alfred Auger, had been killed earlier that morning.

24

SPAD VII (serial unknown) of Lt François Battesti, N73, Bergues, July 1917

Corsican-born François Battesti flew Caudron G4s prior to joining N73. Scoring three victories while flying SPAD VIIs with GC12, he remained with SPA73 after it became the nucleus of GC19. Battesti claimed a further three victories flying SPAD XIIIs and one while flying the cannon-armed SPAD XII.

25

SPAD VII (serial unknown) of Cpl Charles J Biddle, N73, St Eloi, August 1917

One of several American volunteers in N73, Charles John Biddle initially saw combat flying SPAD VIIs, but was flying a new SPAD XIII by the time he scored his first victory on 5 December 1917. Later transferring to the 103rd Aero Squadron, with whom he scored his second victory, Biddle ultimately used his experience, and the tactics he learned under Albert Deullin, to excel as commander of the 13th Aero Squadron, with which unit he brought his total to eight. He finished the war as a major in command of the 4th Pursuit Group.

26

SPAD VII (serial unknown) of Adjutant-Chef François Bergot, N73, St Eloi, summer 1917

A former member of the 2e *Régiment des Chasseurs* and *escadrille* N49, Bergot joined N73 in July 1916, and was credited with the destruction of enemy aircraft on 17 and 23 November. After serving in N38 from 6 to 30 January 1917, he returned to N73, claiming probable victories on 22 April and 2 May. Bergot received the *Médaille Militaire* as a result of these successes on 10 July, and promotion to sous-lieutenant followed on 14 October.

27

SPAD XIII S501 of Lt Albert Deullin, SPA73, St Eloi, September 1917

As one of the leading Stork aces, Deullin was among the first French pilots to receive a SPAD XIII, which Guynemer is believed to have 'borrowed' and damaged on 10 September. S501's darker-than-usual fuselage in photographs suggests that it was refinished as well as repaired by the time Deullin flew it, possibly to score his 18th victory on 27 September, followed by a Pfalz D III on 8 November. Promoted to *capitaine* in October, Deullin was commanding GC19 when he scored his 20th, and last, victory on 19 May 1918.

28

SPAD XIII (serial unknown) of Cpl Frank L Baylies, N73, Bergues, November 1917

Joining N73 on 17 November 1917, Cpl Frank Leaman Baylies described his assigned aeroplane as a SPAD XIII with the number '13', adding, 'cannot afford to be superstitious – nothing like being a fatalist'. He spent his month with Deullin's *escadrille* accumulating experience, but following his transfer to SPA3, 'Jules' Baylies became that squadron's leading ace of 1918, scoring 12 victories before being shot down and killed by a Fokker Dr I of *Jasta* 19 on 22 June.

29

SPAD VII S1832 of MdL Louis Paoli, N73, Bergues, November 1917

The cousin of Lt François Battesti, Paoli became disorientated and landed in the neutral Netherlands in this SPAD, which fell into Dutch hands intact. Paoli later escaped internment and rejoined SPA73, only to be killed in action on 22 August 1918.

30

SPAD VII (serial unknown) of Sous-Lt Auguste Ledeuil, N103, Manoncourt-en-Vermois, March 1917

In addition to N103's red star insignia, Ledeuil's SPAD VII featured a crescent, star and two prominent cockades on the tailplane. He had brought his score to a tantalising four when he was brought down and taken prisoner on 3 March 1917, his demise being credited to Vzfw Friedrich Altemeier of *Jasta* 24.

31

SPAD VII S1461 of Sous-Lt René Fonck, N103, Bonnemaison, summer 1917

Note this aircraft's extra perforations forward of the cowling louvres to aid in cooling the engine. Just visible on the upper wing is N103's old red star insignia, and the fuselage side shows Fonck's red 'IX' superimposed on the overpainted, earlier, 'XV'.

32

SPAD XIII (serial unknown) of Sgt Phelps Collins, SPA103, Beauzée-sur-Aire, January 1918

One of several American members of N103, Phelps Collins was flying a SPAD VII when he downed an Albatros on 14 October 1917, but was photographed alongside this Blériot-built SPAD XIII shortly before leaving the *escadrille* on 7 January 1918. Transferring to the 103rd Aero Squadron, Collins apparently passed out during a high-altitude patrol and fell into a fatal spin on 12 March 1918.

33

SPAD XIII (serial unknown) of Sgt Pierre Schmitter, SPA103, Hétomesnil, spring 1918

Although it did not produce as many aces as other *escadrilles* in GC12, SPA103 had the second highest score overall in the *Aviation Française*. One of those pilots who contributed to that record beside Fonck, Pierre Schmitter was credited with three victories.

34
SPAD XIII (serial unknown) of Capitaine Joseph Battle, SPA103, Hétomesnil, spring 1918
Capitaine Battle had one previous victory to his credit, with SPA77, when he took command of SPA103 on 27 March 1918 – and was wounded in the foot the following day. Returning to combat as soon as he recovered, Battle resumed his scoring with a balloon on 22 August, and finished the war with a total of four victories.

35
SPAD XII S445 of Sous-Lt René Fonck, SPA103, Hétomesnil, May 1918
Fonck downed his first enemy aeroplane using a SPAD XII on 19 May 1918, and he went on to claim ten more victories, of which seven were confirmed, while flying the Cannon SPAD.

36
SPAD XIII S4816 of Sgt Jean Laffray, SPA103, Ferme de la Noblette, October 1918
Although the self-absorbed René Fonck was widely unpopular in GC12, he had his share of partisans in SPA103, including Jean Laffray, whose post-war memoirs praised him for the example he set and the pride he reflected on the *escadrille*. Photographed beside a Levasseur-built SPAD XIII, Laffray scored no confirmed successes of his own during his service in SPA103.

37
SPAD XIII (serial unknown) of Sous-Lt Louis Coudouret, SPA103, Ferme de la Noblette, late 1918
Coudouret damaged this Adolph Bernard-built machine in a landing accident in April 1919, but it cannot be certain whether he regularly flew it during the war. There was also at least one photograph taken of René Fonck standing beside the fighter, either before or after the crack-up, but throughout 1918 his regular SPAD XIII, like his SPAD XII, bore the numeral 'VI'. Already credited with five enemy aeroplanes destroyed while flying with other units – including three over Russia with N581 – Coudouret scored his final victory in concert with Sgt Robert B Hoeber, a Lafayette Flying Corps member of SPA103, on 2 June 1918.

38
SPAD XIII (serial unknown) of Lt Bernard Barny de Romanet, SPA167, Ferme de la Noblette, late autumn 1918
Based on what little material is available, Bernard Barny de Romanet's SPAD has been reconstructed here marked with the usual leader's number, '1'. Although SPA167's combat career only lasted for about a month and a half, N37 veteran de Romanet led it extraordinarily well. Indeed, the unit scored ten victories (eight of which were credited to him, bringing his wartime total to 18) without a single combat loss. Tragically, de Romanet was killed in a flying accident on 23 September 1921.

39
SPAD XIII (serial unknown) of Sous-Lt Emile Antoine Villard, SPA167, Ferme de la Noblette, late autumn 1918
The only photograph showing a known SPAD XIII of SPA167 features a group of pilots sanding before it, with Sous-Lt Villard sitting on '3's' upper decking, suggesting that it might have been his personal machine – not illogical, given his officer status, and the low number. The cowling, like the numeral on the upper right wing, appears to be white. Villard scored his only victory – a two-seater north of Attigny – in collaboration with Sgt Jean de Lombardon on 29 October 1918.

40
SPAD XIII (serial unknown) of Sous-Lt Joseph Henri Guiguet, SPA167, Ferme de la Noblette, late October 1918
No photograph of Guiguet's last SPAD exists, but his notes and description allowed enough for a speculative reconstruction of *"P'tit Jo V"*, the SPAD XIII in which he shared in the destruction of an enemy two-seater with de Romanet on 24 October 1918, placing Guiguet in the ranks of GC12's aces at long last.

BIBLIOGRAPHY

BATTESTI, FRANÇOIS, *Les Cigognes de Brocard au Combat*, La Pensée Universelle, Paris, 1975

BIDDLE, MAJ CHARLES J, *Fighting Airman – The Way of the Eagle*, Ace Books, New York, NY, 1968

CHASSARD, MARC, *René Dorme et Joseph Guiguet – La Guerre Aérienne de Deux As*, Éditions aux Arts, Lyon, France, 2002

FONCK, CAPTAIN RENÉ, edited by Stanley M Ulanoff, *Ace of Aces*, pp 106–107, Doubleday & Co, Inc, Garden City, NY, 1967

FRANKS, NORMAN L R, FRANK W BAILEY AND RUSSELL GUEST, *Above the Lines*, Grub Street, London, 1993

FRANKS, NORMAN L R, AND FRANK W BAILEY, *Over the Front*, Grub Street, London, 1992

FRANKS, NORMAN, FRANK W BAILEY AND RICK DUIVEN, *The Jasta War Chronology*, Grub Street, London, 1998

FRANKS, NORMAN L R, AND FRANK W BAILEY, *The Storks*, Grub Street, London, 1998

GUTTMAN, JON, '"Monsieur Moniteur", Cigogne: Interview with Louis Risacher'. *Cross & Cockade International Journal*, Vol 20 No 2, Summer 1989

HYLANDS, DENNIS, *Georges Guynemer*, Albatros Productions, Ltd, Berkhamstead, Herts, 1987

KROLL, HEINRICH, 'A Fighter Pilot on the Western Front', *Cross & Cockade (USA) Journal*, Vol 14, No 2, p 181, Summer 1983

La Vie Aérienne Illustrée, 1917–18

PORRET, DANIEL, *Les 'As' français de la Grande Guerre*, Service Historique de l'Armée de l'Air, Château de Vincennes, 1983

TÄGER HANNES, 'A Man For "Sonnefilme", Rudolf Windisch', *Over the Front*, Vol 17, No 3, p 214, Fall 2002

UDET, ERNST, *Ace of the Iron Cross*, Arco Publishing, Inc, New York, NY, 1981

WOOLLEY, CHARLES, 'Pages du Gloire: A Brief History of Escadrille 3', *Cross & Cockade (USA) Journal*, Vol 15 No 1, pp 27-62, Spring 1974

INDEX

Figures in **bold** refer to illustrations.